CHINA IN THE 21ST CENTURY

# CHINA INVESTMENT CORPORATION

# CHINA'S KEY SOVEREIGN WEALTH FUND AND CHINESE INVESTMENT ISSUES

# CHINA IN THE 21ST CENTURY

Additional books in this series can be found on Nova's website under the Series tab.

Additional E-books in this series can be found on Nova's website under the E-book tab.

CHINA IN THE 21ST CENTURY

# CHINA INVESTMENT CORPORATION

## CHINA'S KEY SOVEREIGN WEALTH FUND AND CHINESE INVESTMENT ISSUES

INES HEMBRECHT
EDITOR

nova publishers
*New York*

For permission to use material from this book please contact us:
Telephone 631-231-7269; Fax 631-231-8175
Web Site: http://www.novapublishers.com



**Library of Congress Cataloging-in-Publication Data**

ISBN: 978-1-62808-913-4

*Published by Nova Science Publishers, Inc. †New York*

# CONTENTS

# PREFACE

Over the past decade, sovereign wealth funds (SWFs) have proliferated and have increased their role in the international economy. China now has four SWFs and accounts for one-fifth of global SWF assets. China Investment Corp. (CIC), China's flagship SWF, has increased its assets from $200 billion to an estimated $500 billion in just five years as a result of funding and other support from the Chinese government. This book examines the operations and investment strategy of CIC. It also considers how China's SWFs are being regulated in the United States and internationally. The book builds on hearings and research conducted by the U.S.-China Economic and Security Review Commission (USCC) in 2008. At the time, CIC had just purchased equity in Wall Street firms Morgan Stanley and Blackstone. Since then, CIC has bought shares in dozens of publicly traded U.S. companies, partnered with U.S. fund managers, and provided capital to U.S. energy companies.

Chapter 1 – Following its establishment, CIC signed on to the Santiago Principles, a set of transparency and governance recommendations for SWFs promulgated by the International Monetary Fund (IMF). And yet, questions remain about the objectives and behavior of China's sovereign investors. SWFs are generally based in small, wealthy economies, such as Singapore and Norway. Most are commodity exporters who use SWFs to counter price volatility and transfer wealth to future generations. In contrast, China is the world's second-largest economy and largest commodity importer. It has low per capita income and is a net recipient of foreign investment.

China's SWFs are partly a product of China's economic rise and a government strategy to promote outbound investment. China's industry-heavy, urbanizing economy has registered rising trade deficits in commodities, as well as declining terms of trade due to a lack of control over more profitable industries. SWFs, like other Chinese investors, can mitigate these problems by taking direct equity positions in overseas industries, thereby stabilizing supply and partaking in profits.

But China's SWFs have also served to generate returns on the country's savings. China has controlled its capital accounts and exchange rate in order to promote exports and subsidize domestic production. This policy requires the central bank to pump money into the domestic economy and to deposit dollars received in trade into low-yielding U.S. Treasury securities. That has created inflationary pressures and an inherent risk that the dollar reserves will lose value. The government has used state-sponsored investments to earn a higher return on the dollar reserves than would be provided by U.S. treasuries.

Chapter 2 – Testimony of Thilo Hanemann, Research Director, Rhodium Group LLC.

Chapter 3 – Testimony of Derek Scissors, Senior Research Fellow in Asia Economics, The Heritage Foundation.

Chapter 4 – Testimony of Andrew Szamosszegi, Principal, Capital Trade, Inc.

Chapter 5 – Testimony of Elizabeth Drake, Partner, Law Offices of Stewart and Stewart.

Chapter 6 – Testimony of Mark E. Plotkin, Partner, Covington & Burling LLP. Testimony of Mark E. Plotkin, Partner, Covington & Burling LLP.

In: China Investment Corporation
Editor: Ines Hembrecht
ISBN: 978-1-62808-913-4


*Chapter 1*

# CHINA INVESTMENT CORPORATION: RECENT DEVELOPMENTS IN PERFORMANCE, STRATEGY, AND GOVERNANCE*

***Iacob N. Koch-Weser and Owen D. Haacke***

## EXECUTIVE SUMMARY

Over the past decade, sovereign wealth funds (SWFs) have proliferated and have increased their role in the international economy. China now has four SWFs and accounts for one-fifth of global SWF assets. China Investment Corp. (CIC), China's flagship SWF, has increased its assets from $200 billion to an estimated $500 billion in just five years as a result of funding and other support from the Chinese government.

This report examines the operations and investment strategy of CIC. It also considers how China's SWFs are being regulated in the United States and internationally. The report builds on hearings and research conducted by the U.S.-China Economic and Security Review Commission (USCC) in 2008. At the time, CIC had just purchased equity in Wall Street firms Morgan Stanley and Blackstone. Since then, CIC has bought shares in dozens of publicly

---

* This is an edited, reformatted and augmented version of the U.S.-China Economic and Security Review Commission, dated June 13, 2013.

traded U.S. companies, partnered with U.S. fund managers, and provided capital to U.S. energy companies.

Following its establishment, CIC signed on to the Santiago Principles, a set of transparency and governance recommendations for SWFs promulgated by the International Monetary Fund (IMF). And yet, questions remain about the objectives and behavior of China's sovereign investors. SWFs are generally based in small, wealthy economies, such as Singapore and Norway. Most are commodity exporters who use SWFs to counter price volatility and transfer wealth to future generations. In contrast, China is the world's second-largest economy and largest commodity importer. It has low per capita income and is a net recipient of foreign investment.

China's SWFs are partly a product of China's economic rise and a government strategy to promote outbound investment. China's industry-heavy, urbanizing economy has registered rising trade deficits in commodities, as well as declining terms of trade due to a lack of control over more profitable industries. SWFs, like other Chinese investors, can mitigate these problems by taking direct equity positions in overseas industries, thereby stabilizing supply and partaking in profits.

But China's SWFs have also served to generate returns on the country's savings. China has controlled its capital accounts and exchange rate in order to promote exports and subsidize domestic production. This policy requires the central bank to pump money into the domestic economy and to deposit dollars received in trade into low-yielding U.S. Treasury securities. That has created inflationary pressures and an inherent risk that the dollar reserves will lose value. The government has used state-sponsored investments to earn a higher return on the dollar reserves than would be provided by U.S. treasuries.

China's SWF strategy is far from coordinated. While most countries have one or two SWFs, China has four – CIC, SAFE Investment Company (SAFEIC), National Social Security Fund (NSSF), and China-Africa Development Fund (CADF) – each established to serve separate interests among branches of the Chinese government. These SWFs must compete for access to foreign exchange reserves with state-sponsored banks and enterprises. The Ministry of Finance (MOF) has advocated that CIC become China's primary outbound investor and has exercised control over the fund's management. On the other hand, the People's Bank of China (PBOC), China's central bank, prefers instead to distribute dollar reserves prudently among several state investors or to manage them through its own subsidiaries.

These disagreements may explain why CIC, China's only officially recognized SWF, has no defined strategy to guide its operations. The fund has only been capitalized twice – with $200 billion in 2007 and $30 billion in 2011 – and has no stable funding mechanism. Because CIC is not owned or outsourced by the PBOC, it has been financed through special government bonds issued by MOF, which has created a significant debt burden for CIC. CIC has been able to grow its assets primarily because it owns stakes in China's major commercial banks. These banks have rapidly grown their assets over the past decade, in part by listing on China's stock exchanges.

CIC has also been ambivalent about its investment strategy. Since incurring losses on Wall Street in 2008, the fund has recruited more staff, reorganized its investment departments, and established offices in Toronto and Hong Kong. CIC has partnered with external fund managers, exacting favorable terms from financial institutions in need of cash during a global economic downturn. But CIC is under public pressure to generate high returns on an annual basis, to justify more funding. As a result, it has taken significant risks and registered volatile returns on its international portfolio.

Counter to its claims of being strictly profit driven, CIC has pursued strategic objectives. It has diverted capital from its outbound portfolio in order to shore up the balance sheets and share values of the domestic banks it owns. CIC has also purchased shares of Chinese state-owned enterprises (SOEs) listed in Hong Kong. Moreover, the fund has worked with international companies in strategic sectors, such as oil and gas, and coordinated these activities with China's state-owned banks and enterprises. Although CIC claims to be a passive investor, it has taken a seat on the board of U.S. energy giant AES and other foreign firms. It has promoted China's economic diplomacy by cooperating with SWFs from other countries and by enhancing China's ownership of assets in advanced economies.

In terms of governance, CIC maintains very close ties to the state. The fund is registered as a wholly state-owned company under China's Company Law, and is required to have a Communist Party Committee. Only three out of 25 board members are not current or former government officials. In 2013, the fund was part of China's once-in-a-decade leadership transition: CIC Chairman Lou Jiwei became the Minister of Finance, and his successor has yet to be named.

To date, international efforts to regulate SWFs have fallen short. Although CIC participated in drafting the Santiago Principles and signed on in 2008, it has failed to meet all of the recommendations in terms of disclosure of its domestic investments, shareholder relations, and auditing practices. Moreover, China's other sovereign investors, which in many cases are less transparent, have not even signed on. CIC and other SWFs are currently subject only to domestic regulation, while international regulation is still vague and nonbinding.

In the United States, the question of how to treat incoming investment from China's sovereign investors remains unresolved. Some policymakers support lenient treatment to encourage foreign investment, while others worry about national security. In terms of actual regulation, the Committee on Foreign Investment in the United States (CFIUS) has so far reviewed only one investment by CIC, because the fund has been careful to keep its equity stakes small. A revised statute could make more of CIC's transactions subject to CFIUS review. The Securities and Exchange Commission (SEC) and Federal Reserve (Fed) have been more active in reviewing financial sector operations by CIC and its banking subsidiaries. Although with some conditionality, the Fed has approved all of the proposals, exempting CIC from many of the rules under the Bank Holding Company Act (BHCA). The Internal Revenue Service (IRS), for its part, has largely exempted SWFs from paying U.S. corporate income taxes by classifying them as a "foreign government."

China's SWFs help perpetuate a broader structural imbalance between deficit and surplus countries in the world economy. Besides improving the regulation of these funds, the U.S. government could continue to push for economic reform in China.

## INTRODUCTION

Over the past decade, sovereign wealth funds have become major actors in the global financial sector. Like hedge funds, SWFs lie outside the traditional banking system, and many critics argue that they are not sufficiently transparent. There is also an inherent risk that state-sponsored actors will pursue noncommercial objectives; for instance, by acquiring strategic assets in advanced economies. In the United States, these issues became apparent in February 2006, when Congress blocked the sale of port management businesses in six major U.S. seaports to a state-owned enterprise from the United Arab Emirates, citing national security concerns. Misgivings increased in 2007, when several SWFs acquired interests in Wall Street banks. Among them was China Investment Corp. (CIC), China's newly established SWF, which invested billions in private equity fund Blackstone and investment bank Morgan Stanley.

In 2008, the U.S.-China Economic and Security Review Commission (USCC) became one of the first institutions to address the policy implications of outbound investment by China's SWFs. The Commission received testimony from the Treasury Department and the Peterson Institute for International Economics, among other experts.* The Commissioners later traveled to Beijing to speak with the leadership of CIC, China's flagship sovereign wealth fund. In its 2008 Report to Congress, the Commission expressed concern about China's SWFs, due to "uncertainty about the Chinese government and the Chinese Communist Party's motivations, strategies, and possible impacts on market stability and national security". It also predicted that China's sovereign investors would establish a substantial and long-term presence in the U.S. economy.[1]

China's SWFs now rank among the largest in the world. They have purchased equities on the U.S. stock exchange, partnered with U.S. fund managers, and acquired large stakes in U.S. financial services and energy companies. The United States is just a small part of the global investments of these funds. At the same time, China's SWFs remain closely tied to the Chinese government. During China's once-in-a-decade leadership transition in March 2013, CIC's Chairman Lou Jiwei became the Minister of Finance and has yet to be replaced at CIC. In turn, the former Minister of Finance, Xie Xuren, was appointed to head NSSF, another one of China's four SWFs.

This report analyzes China's SWFs, with a particular focus on CIC. It poses three questions:

(1) How have China's SWFs expanded? What role do they play in China's economic policy and management of foreign exchange reserves?
(2) To what extent is CIC a commercial or strategic investor, in terms of its investments and governance structure?
(3) How transparent and accountable are China's SWFs, and how well are they being regulated by the U.S. government and the international community?

The report draws on a wealth of data that have become available in recent years. CIC has published detailed annual reports since 2009. The policy literature has expanded, thanks in part to the Sovereign Wealth Fund Initiative at Tufts University. Academics have analyzed SWFs in depth, especially

* Refer to the USCC's February 7, 2008, "Hearing on the Implications of Sovereign Wealth Fund Investments for National Security." Transcripts available at http://www.uscc.gov/hearings/2008hearings/hr08_02_07.php.

during the global financial crisis. Financial journalists have produced timely reports, and CIC's managers have given several interviews to the press.

The report's main finding is that the Chinese government still has no apparent strategy to guide SWF investments. CIC, the only SWF officially acknowledged by Beijing, lacks a stable funding mechanism and competes with other state-sponsored investors. It holds assets in both the domestic and international economy and pursues both commercial and strategic objectives.

The report is structured in five sections. Section 1 compares China's SWFs to other countries and considers the Chinese government's policy objectives. Sections 2 and 3 examine CIC's efforts to access funding, increase profits, and promote the government's strategic objectives. Sections 4 and 5 analyze governance and regulatory issues.

# SECTION 1: SOVEREIGN WEALTH FUNDS IN CHINA'S ECONOMIC POLICY

## China as an Outlier in the SWF Sector

SWFs date back to the 1950s but have proliferated since the 1990s. Of the 64 SWFs listed by the Sovereign Wealth Fund Institute (SWFI), a private consultancy, over half were established since 2001. According to CityUK, a private consultancy, SWFs doubled their share of the global fund management industry in 2003-11, exceeding the assets of hedge funds and private equity combined. CityUK forecasts SWF assets to be twice as large as the United Kingdom's gross domestic product (GDP) by year-end 2013.[2]

Several factors explain this growth. Sovereign wealth has traditionally been used to stabilize revenues from the sale of commodities, such as oil and gas, and to transfer commodity-based wealth to future generations. Over the past decade, commodity exporters have also benefited from a secular rise in commodity prices, due in no small measure to China's booming demand. At the same time, SWFs have grown in countries that do not export many commodities.[3] According to SWFI data, noncommodity funds increased their share of SWF assets from 28 percent to 43 percent in 2001-11. The rationale for SWFs in these countries is less obvious, since the economy is not as susceptible to market volatility and does not depend on a finite resource. The main reason is that, after being devastated by capital flight during the Asian Financial Crisis in 1997-98, many Asian governments have used their trade surpluses to build up much larger dollar reserves.[4]

Countries with large foreign exchange reserves tend to park their holdings in U.S. treasuries, which are considered a safe haven. The purchase of treasuries also supports spending in the U.S. economy, which can boost U.S. demand for exports from SWF countries. However, in the face of a weakening dollar and large external deficits in the United States, these countries have begun to use SWFs to diversify a portion of their holdings into higher-risk, higher-return assets. In the wake of the global financial crisis, there have also been attractive opportunities to buy undervalued assets in advanced economies.[5]

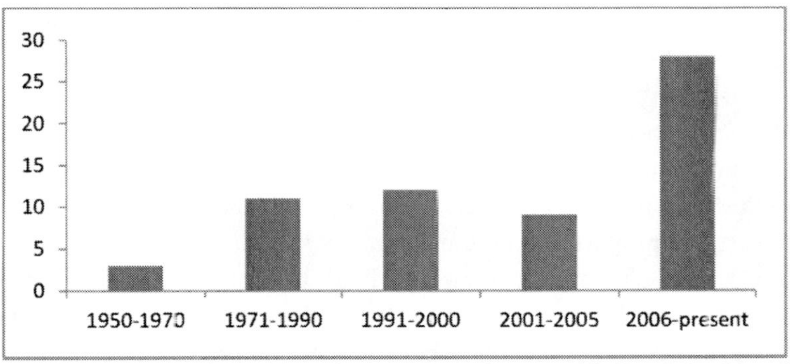


Source: Sovereign Wealth Fund Institute, "Sovereign Wealth Fund Rankings" (Las Vegas, NV). http://www.swfinstitute.org/fund-rankings/.

Figure 1-1. Number of Sovereign Wealth Funds Established by Time Period.

**Table 1-1. Growth of Sovereign Wealth Funds: Commodity vs. Noncommodity**

| | Absolute (US$ bn) | | CAGR (%) | Share of total (%) | |
|---|---|---|---|---|---|
| | 2001 | 2012 | 2001-2012 | 2001 | 2012 |
| Non-commodity | 293 | 2,214 | 20% | 28% | 43% |
| Commodity | 765 | 2,991 | 13% | 72% | 57% |
| Total | 1,058 | 5,205 | 16% | | |

Sources: The City-UK estimates. http://stagingtcuk.positive-technology.com/research/our-work/reports-list/fund-management-2010/; Sovereign Wealth Fund Institute.

Although China broadly conforms to these trends, it is an outlier among SWF countries. One aspect is its sheer size. The assets of CIC increased from $200 billion to an estimated $500 billion since the fund's creation in 2007, making it the world's fifth-largest SWF. Although the Chinese government recognizes only CIC as an official SWF, the Sovereign Wealth Fund Institute, an independent consultancy, has identified four Chinese SWFs, and ranks them as the third (SAFEIC), fifth (CIC), eleventh (NSSF), and forty-third (CADF) largest in the world.[*] According to this measure, China by 2011 accounted for one-quarter of global SWF assets, the largest of any country.

Behind these SWFs are China's foreign exchange reserves, which are by far the largest in the world. China is also the largest holder of U.S. treasuries. Even relative to China's huge economy, its reserves are abnormally high. In 2007, the year CIC was founded, China needed an estimated $670 billion of prudential reserves,[†] but its actual reserves were $1.6 trillion.[6] Although its reserve growth has slowed in the intervening years, China continues to have a vast surplus to invest.

China is also an outlier in institutional terms. Most SWFs are based in small, wealthy economies, like the Gulf States, Norway, and Singapore. When such states become net exporters, their current account surpluses quickly become large in proportion to the national economy. This structural constraint incentivizes the use of a centralized fund to make profitable, long-term investments overseas.[7] In contrast, China is the world's second-largest economy and the second-leading recipient of foreign direct investment (FDI). China is also not wealthy; in 2011, the World Bank ranked it ninety-ninth worldwide in per capita income.[8] In theory, it should be more difficult for China to accumulate excess reserves, and there should be ample opportunity to make welfare- enhancing investments domestically.

---

[*] Experts continue to debate what type of public fund should qualify as an SWF, since the term was only coined in 2005. That has caused some confusion. A fair definition, provided by Ashby Monk, is that SWFs are generally public funds that owe liabilities only to their sponsoring government and invest their assets according to the sponsoring government's interests and objectives. For a detailed analysis, see Appendix Table A-1.

[†] A common benchmark for prudential reserves is that they suffice to pay off foreign loans; to protect against an outflow of speculative "hot money"; to pay off three months' worth of imports; and to intervene in foreign exchange markets to keep the domestic currency within a certain band. Economists often refer to the Guidotti-Greenspan rule, which states that a country's reserves should equal short-term external debt (one year or less maturity), implying a ratio of reserves-to-short-term debt of 1. The rationale is that countries should have enough reserves to resist a massive withdrawal of short-term foreign capital. Dani Rodrik, "The Social Cost of Foreign Exchange Reserves," *International Economic Journal* 20:3 (September 2006): 255-59.

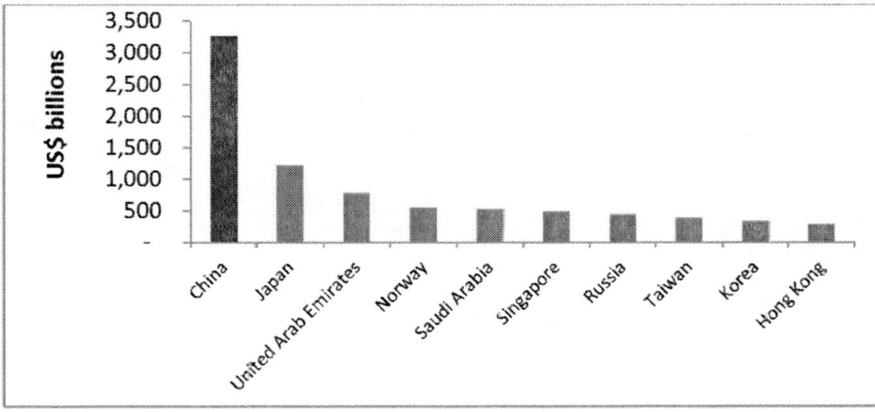


Source: C. Fred Bergsten and Joseph E. Gagnon, "Currency Manipulation, the US Economy, and the Global Economic Order" (Washington, DC: The Peterson Institute for International Economics Policy Brief 12-25 (December 2012).

Figure 1-2. Top-Ten Countries by Foreign Exchange Reserves, 2011.

While most countries have just one or two SWFs, China established four entities between 1997 and 2007. Each is unique in terms of its legal basis, governance, and mandate:

- *SAFE Investment Company (SAFEIC)** (est. 1997). SAFEIC is a limited company registered in Hong Kong, prior to the handover of the island to Mainland China. It constitutes one of four overseas investment arms of the State Administration of Foreign Exchange (SAFE). SAFE is the branch of the People's Bank of China, China's central bank, which exclusively manages China's foreign exchange reserves. SAFEIC's primary objective is to retain the value of China's foreign exchange by making portfolio investments overseas.
- *National Social Security Fund (NSSF)* (est. 2000). Established by the State Council, under the auspices of the Ministry of Social Security, NSSF is a public pension fund under China's Social Insurance Law. Its objective is to maintain the real value of public pension proceeds as a means to support future social security expenditures. NSSF can invest 20 percent of its funds outside China.
- *China Investment Corp. (CIC)* (est. 2007). Like SAFEIC, CIC is a "company" but is registered as a state-owned enterprise under China's

* In China, SAFEIC is referred to as "Hua'an Guoji Touzi Gongsi (华安国际投资公司)".

Company Law. Unlike SAFEIC and NSSF, it is not a legal subsidiary of any government agency and reports like a ministry directly to the State Council, the highest administrative body. Under CIC's Articles of Association, five government agencies – PBOC, SAFE, the Ministry of Finance, the Ministry of Commerce (MOFCOM), and the National Development and Reform Commission (NDRC) – are allowed to nominate one nonexecutive director to CIC's board. CIC has neither a direct funding mechanism nor any statutory limit on its outbound investments.

- *China-Africa Development Fund (CADF)* (est. 2007). CADF is a small fund set up to foster economic ties between China and Africa. It functions as a branch of China Development Bank (CDB), China's largest policy bank, though various government ministries are represented on its board. It is worth noting that CDB is majority owned by Central Huijin, the domestic subsidiary of CIC (See Section 2 for details).

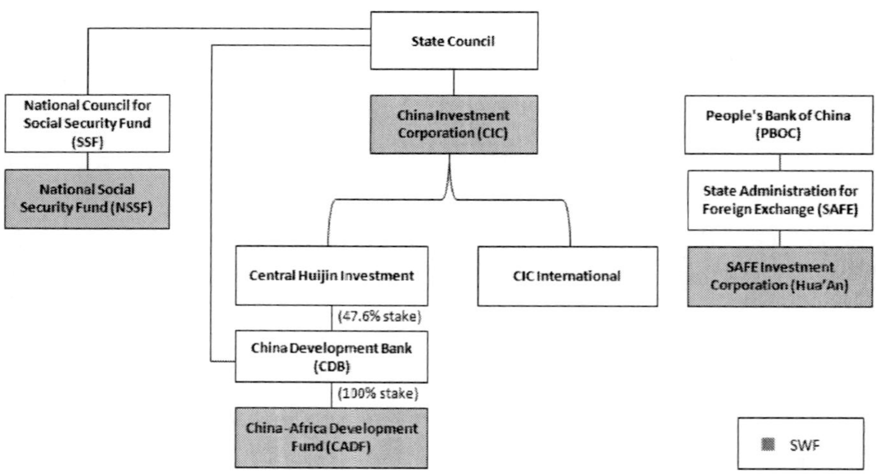


Source: "National Social Security Fund [Quanguo Baozhang Jijin]," National Council for Social Security Fund website, http://www.ssf.gov.cn/jj/qgsbjj/201205/t20120507_3993.html; *China Investment Corporation, Annual Report 2011* (Beijing: 2012), p. 11; China Development Bank, *2011 Annual Report* (Beijing: 2012), p. 147; "SAFE Investment Company," Sovereign Wealth Fund Institute. http://www.swfinstitute.org/swfs/safe-investment-company/.

Figure 1-3. Sovereign Wealth Funds in China's Administrative Structure.

## Domestic Factors: Industrial and Monetary Policy

To some extent, China's SWFs are a product of the country's economic rise and a government strategy to promote outbound investment. Since the advent of the Reform and Opening Up policy in 1978, China's GDP growth has far exceeded the world average, on the basis of an export-oriented growth model. In a maturing economy, producers and investors are more integrated into global markets and have accumulated capital to invest overseas.

At the same time, China's industry-heavy, urbanizing economy has registered rising trade deficits in commodities, as well as declining terms of trade[*] due to a lack of control over more profitable industries. SWFs, like other Chinese investors, can reduce these problems by taking direct stakes in foreign enterprises, thereby stabilizing China's supply of resources and accruing profits in more lucrative sectors. Due to the government's quasi-monopoly control over outbound investment,[†] there is also evidence of coordinated outbound investment. In its 10th Five-Year Plan (2001-05), the government introduced the "go global" directive, which encouraged Chinese companies and funds to invest overseas to acquire resources, technology, and know-how.[‡] The directive gained further momentum during the global financial crisis, which provided a rare opportunity to buy undervalued assets in foreign markets.[§] Since 2008, China's outbound investment has grown steadily and has begun to outpace inbound investment.

---

[*] Terms of trade is the ratio of export unit value to import unit value. A high ratio signals that the value of a country's exports per unit is greater than its imports per unit, meaning that the products a country sells overseas are more expensive than the products in imports. Countries with high ratios are regarded to be at an advantage, and have the ability to pay for more imports by selling a smaller amount of exports. Countries with a low ratio, however, need to sell more exports to buy the same amount of imports.

[†] Although the Chinese government has released decentralized approvals, investments that require over $50 million in foreign currency still require approval of the NDRC and State Council. Moreover, state-owned companies have been investing heavily overseas. For example, according to statistics from Rhodium Group, over 60 percent of China's cumulative foreign direct investment in the United States originates from companies in which the Chinese government has a stake over 20 percent. "China Goes Global: Examining China's Outbound Investment," China Insights (Benesch, Friedlander, Coplan & Aronoff LLP: 2010), p.4 http://www.beneschlaw.com/Files/Publication/58b1c8f1-d679-4051-b50f4631d1cac3b4/Presentation/PublicationAttachment/309b0f83-98ba-4ee8-b03f46526897d787/January_2010.pdf; Rhodium Group, China Investment Monitor through Q1:2013 (New York, NY: 2013).http://rhgroup.net/interactive/china-investment-monitor.

[‡] The "go global" strategy became an official priority of the Chinese government in 2000 when it was included in the 10th Five Year Plan (2001-05).

[§] In July 2009, Premier Wen Jiabao told a meeting of senior Chinese diplomats that the country's vast foreign currency holdings should be used to help Chinese companies "go global," explicitly linking foreign exchange reserves to outward investment and export promotion.

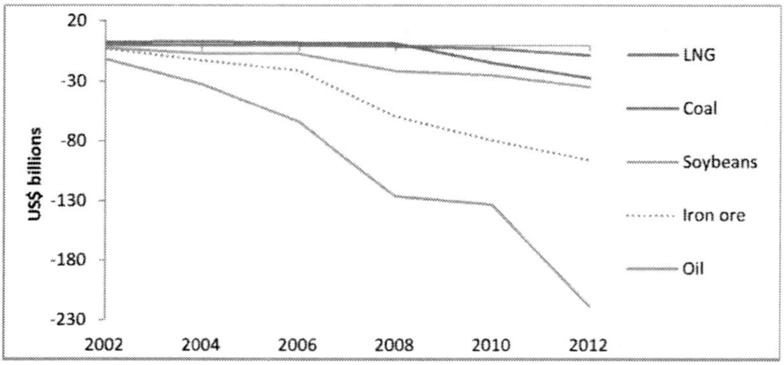


Note: LNG=liquefied natural gas

Source: People's Republic of China, General Administration of Customs (Beijing, China: 2013).

Figure 1-4. China's Growing Deficits in Key Resources.

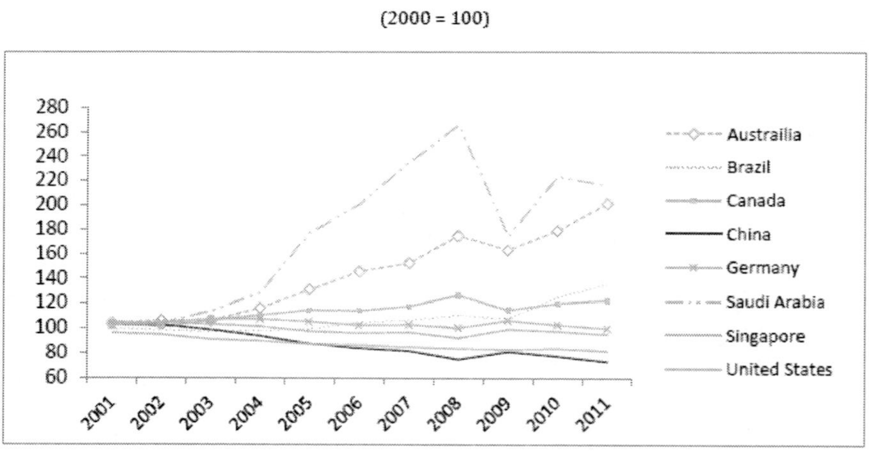


Source: World Bank (Washington, DC: 2013). http://data.worldbank.org/indicator/TT.PRI.MRCH.XD.WD.

Figure 1-5. Net Barter Terms of Trade Index, 2001-2011.

While economic growth and industrial policy have played an important role in the expansion of SWFs, a more salient factor has been China's monetary policy. The years leading up to the creation of CIC in 2007 were

Eiichi Sekine, "China's Foreign Exchange Reserves and China Investment Corporation's Steps towards Diversifying How It Manages Its Portion of Them," *Nomura Journal of Capital Markets* 1:4 (Winter 2009): 1.

formative. Following accession to the World Trade Organization (WTO) in 2001, China opened its markets further to trade and investment and witnessed record levels of dollar inflows. In 2001-06, China's exports vaulted from 23 percent to 39 percent of GDP – an astounding increase, given that real GDP was growing by over 10 percent a year. China also became one of the top three recipients of FDI in the world. As these inflows increased, the central bank came under growing pressure to allow market-based appreciation of the renminbi (RMB) currency, which was set at a fixed rate to the U.S. dollar. Compounding the situation was so-called "hot money," short- term portfolio inflows by investors who speculated that the RMB would increase in value.*

To counteract these pressures, the central bank had to purchase large amounts of foreign exchange and park it in dollar-denominated U.S. treasuries. In the domestic economy, in turn, it had to increase the money supply, causing excess liquidity. To stem inflation, the central bank effectively "soaked up" liquidity by issuing RMB-denominated bonds. Such sterilization proved especially costly when the interest the central bank paid out in RMB exceeded the interest received on U.S. treasuries. There was no easy solution to this problem: Letting the RMB appreciate would reduce the dollar inflows and make it easier to manage the money supply, yet it would also decrease the value of China's dollar holdings and threaten the competitiveness of the export sector. In the summer of 2005, the central bank allowed the currency to appreciate slightly, for the first time since 1994. Yet by 2007, dollar inflows continued unabated, and China began to incur substantial losses on its holdings of U.S. treasuries.[9]

These monetary policy dilemmas were addressed by China's top leadership at the Central Financial Working Conference in January 2007. The leadership concluded that traditional monetary policy tools were not enough to stem rising reserves – China needed to look at options to broaden its investment vehicles to "actively" pursue higher returns on surplus dollar reserves.[10] That led to the establishment of CIC in September of that year. Since 2007, capital inflows have slowed somewhat, and China's currency has appreciated by more than 30 percent in real terms against the dollar. Yet the imperative to diversify China's surplus reserves remains strong.

* The RMB-USD exchange rate was 2.8 in January 1985; 5.22 in January 1990; and 8.7 in January 1994, where it remained until July 2005. Oanda. http://www.oanda.com/currency/historical-rates/.

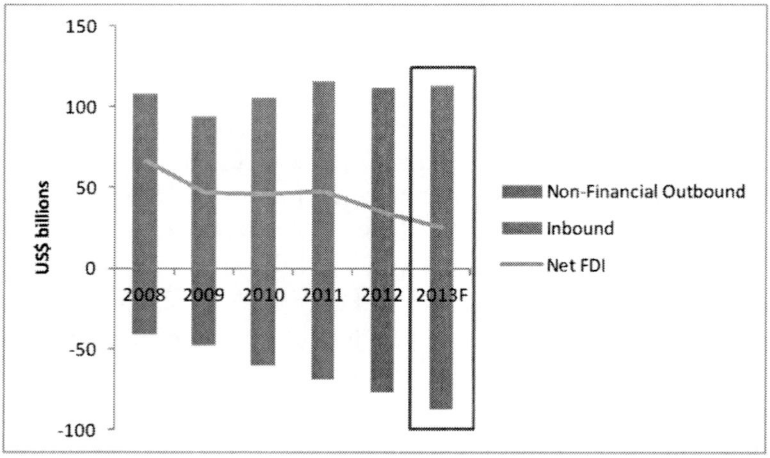


Note: The 2013 forecast is from the National Development and Reform Commission, China's premier planning agency. Outbound investment in the first two months of 2013 exceeded inbound FDI by nearly $1 billion. Bloomberg, "China's Foreign Investment Rebounds as Confidence Returns: Economy,", March 19, 2013. http://www.bloomberg.com/news/2013-03-19/china-s-foreign-investment-gains-for-first-time-in-nine- months.html.

Source: China Ministry of Commerce, via CEIC data.

Figure 1-6. China's Inbound and Outbound Foreign Investment.

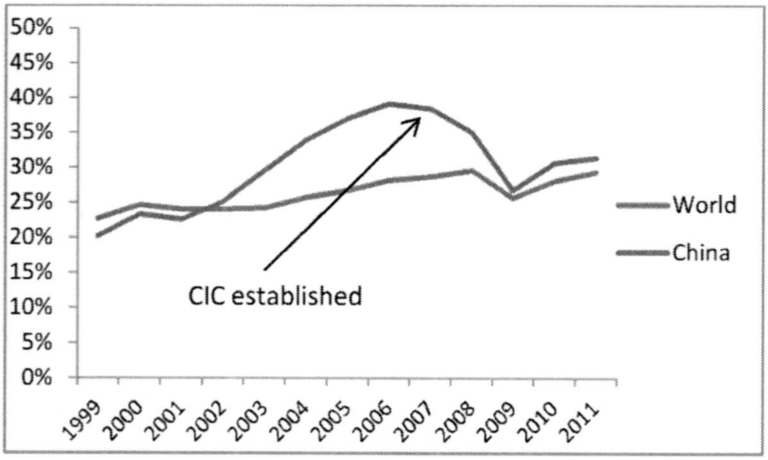


Source: World Bank (Washington, DC: 2012). http://data.worldbank.org/indicator/NE.EXP.GNFS.ZS.

Figure 1-7. Export-to-GDP Ratio, China and the World, 1999-2011.

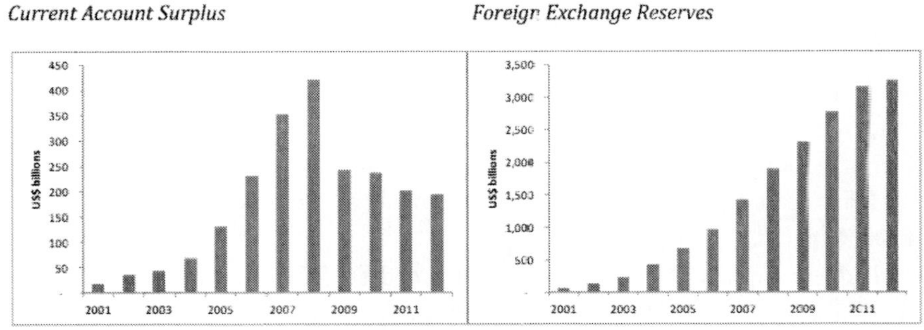


Source: China State Administration of Foreign Exchange, via CEIC data.

Figure 1-8. China's Current Account Surplus and Foreign Exchange Reserves, 2001-2012.

# SECTION 2: THE FUNDING AND GROWTH OF CIC

## Policy Disputes over CIC

### *The Dispute between MOF and the PBOC*

A consensus has formed in the Chinese government about the benefits of state-sponsored outbound investment. Even so, there is considerable disagreement on how this should be done. Extensive state influence in China's economy enables strategic coordination but can also lead to bureaucratic infighting.* Unlike other leading economies, the Ministry of Finance has no say over China's foreign exchange policy, which is under the exclusive jurisdiction of SAFE, a branch of the PBOC.† As China's dollar reserves have

* Academics have offered many theories on the rivalries within China's large bureaucracy. China policy experts Kenneth Lieberthal and Michael Oksenberg in the late 1980s developed the concept of "fragmented authoritarianism". The term essentially refers to a political system that combines a highly complex bureaucracy with one-party rule. China has parallel agencies in the Communist Party, administrative government, and military, each with central and local level representatives. Moreover, agency jurisdictions often overlap, and some – like the State Council and National Development and Reform Commission – are effectively "super-agencies" that have many functions. At the pinnacle of the system is the Communist Party's 25-member Politburo and seven-member Standing Committee. Major decisions are usually made in the Politburo, while less vital issues are settled by lower agencies. See Kenneth Lieberthal and Michael Oksenberg, *Policy Making in China* (Princeton, NJ: Princeton University Press, 1988).

† The bulk of all foreign exchange, earned either by individuals or by enterprises, has to be sold to SAFE in exchange for China's domestic currency, the RMB, at a rate determined by state economic planners. When individuals or enterprises want to purchase foreign exchange,

accumulated, MOF has made increasing efforts to wrest control from SAFE. Some scholars argue that this dispute climaxed during the Central Financial Working Conference in January 2007, when MOF proposed two solutions to managing China's bulging dollar reserves: (1) the creation of a new SWF to diversify China's foreign exchange holdings; and (2) the creation of a Financial Assets Commission that would manage the assets of China's state-owned financial institutions.[11]

Both proposals were a direct affront to the PBOC. On the one hand, its subsidiary SAFE had decades of experience in managing foreign exchange, with fund management arms in Singapore, Hong Kong, London, and New York. The Hong Kong arm quietly evolved into the largest customers for local treasury bond trading desks at banks such as Morgan Stanley. The proposal to set up a Financial Asset Commission was also controversial, because the largest banking assets were being managed directly by PBOC through Central Huijin, a bank holding company established in 2003. [12]

Decisions made at the Financial Work Conference in January 2007 appeared to favor MOF over the PBOC.[*] The Chinese leadership agreed to establish CIC and handed managerial control to MOF. In order to avoid bureaucratic disputes, CIC's articles of association mandated that five major government agencies – including the PBOC and SAFE – nominate one nonexecutive director to CIC's board of directors.[†]Yet the chairmen of CIC's board of directors and board of supervisors were former top officials from MOF and remained in this position in 2007-12.[13] In 2013, CIC Chairman Lou Jiwei vacated his position to become the Minister of Finance. Although his successor is unlikely to come from MOF, day-to-day operations could remain the chief responsibility of incumbent CIC President Gao Xiqing, a Wall Street veteran whom many now view as the international face of the fund (See Section 4 for further discussion of the CIC leadership transition).[14]

---

they have to gain approval from SAFE. These rules were formalized under the Law of the People's Bank of China (1995), which gives the central bank the legal right to own, administer, and manage China's foreign reserves. See Chapter I.5, *Law of the People's Republic of China on the People's Bank of China.* http://www.china.org.cn/business/laws_regulations/2007- 06/22/content_1214826.htm.

[*] U.S. political scientist and China expert Victor Shih has speculated that the MOF proposals were backed by Premier Wen Jiabao, who was in charge of China's Financial Leading Group, and had a close personal relationship with then Vice-Minister of MOF, Lou Jiwei, who became CIC's Chairman. Victor Shih, "Tools of Survival: Sovereign Wealth Funds in Singapore and China," *Geopolitics* 14:2 (2009): 334-35.

[†] Hu Xiaolian served as Non-Executive Director at CIC while serving as Director of SAFE in 2007-09. After she left to become Deputy Governor of the PBOC in 2009, she was replaced by Fang Shangpu, Deputy Administrator of SAFE. China Investment Corp. annual reports 2008-2010.

MOF not only succeeded in establishing and controlling CIC; the PBOC was also compelled in 2007 to relinquish control over Central Huijin, the bank holding company. Surprisingly, Central Huijin's assets were not placed in a new Financial Assets Commission managed by MOF. That appears to have been politically unacceptable for the PBOC. Instead, Central Huijin was sold at a discounted price of $67 billion to CIC in the fall of 2007. In this way, the government retained its stake in the state banks, to be used as tools of policy, while avoiding a controversial decision about whether to hand them to either PBOC or MOF.[15]

Although officially mandated to make outbound investments, CIC became heavily invested in the domestic financial industry. Central Huijin owned major stakes in 18 leading financial institutions, including China's four major commercial banks, largest policy banks, and largest insurance companies. Among these, ten are majority stakes. Indeed, by 2010, CIC's long-term equity investments in domestic banks accounted for over half of its total assets. These domestic holdings also generated massive investment income in 2008 and 2011 that offset losses in the fund's international portfolio.*

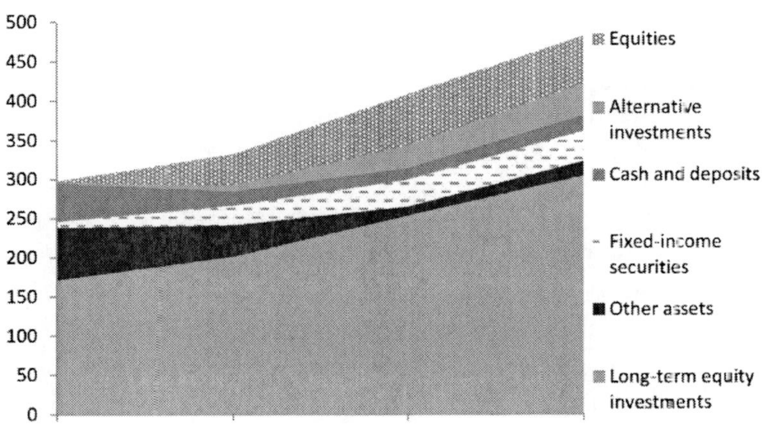


Note: Long-term equity investments are principally comprised of investments by Central Huijin. Source: China Investment Corporation, *2008-2011 Annual Reports* (Beijing, China).

Figure 2-1. CIC Total Asset Distribution ($ billions).

* See Holdings of Central Huijin (Table A-5) and CIC Financials, 2008-11 (Table A-10) in the Appendix.

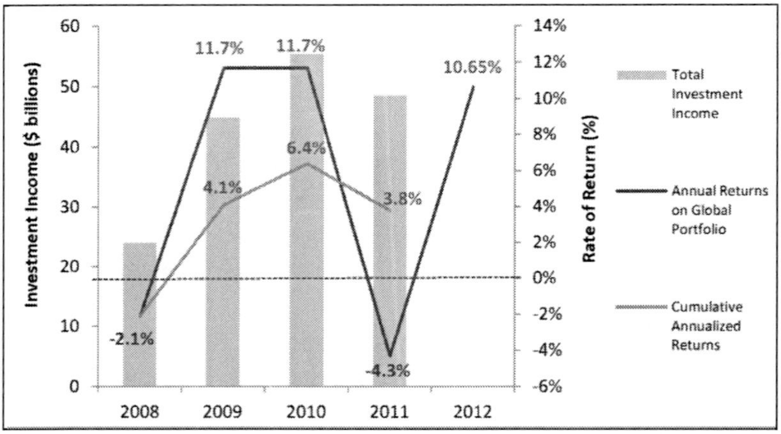


Sources: China Investment Corporation, *2008-2011 Annual Reports* (Beijing, China); *Wall Street Journal*, "China CIC Exec: 2012 Overseas Investment Return Was 10.65%," March 5, 2013. http://online.wsj.com/article/BT-CO-20130305-715944.html.

Figure 2-2. CIC Global Investment Portfolio Annual Returns vs. Total Income.

### *The Funding Dilemma*

The creation of CIC, and its control over domestic banking assets, arguably boosted MOF's influence over monetary policy. Yet CIC inherited serious structural flaws. SWFs are typically established either as legal entities separate from the central bank or as a pool of assets managed by the government. SWFs also tend to have a fixed funding mechanism (e.g., export revenues) and sound rules outlining conditions for the withdrawal of SWF capital, such as fluctuations in commodity prices. In contrast, CIC is registered as an independent, state-owned enterprise. It is neither outsourced to manage funds on the PBOC's behalf, nor a subsidiary of the PBOC. It also has no sound rules regarding the receipt or withdrawal of funds.[16] Indeed, because CIC is classified as a "nonbanking institution," the PBOC is forbidden by law to inject capital into CIC without approval of the State Council, which acts as CIC's official shareholder.[17] The result is that CIC must lobby the State Council and its subordinate ministry, MOF, to appropriate more funding on its behalf.

In March 2011, CIC Executive Vice President Wang Jianxi told the *Wall Street Journal* that the fund was seeking a "clear funding mechanism just like what other, more mature funds have" and noted that CIC was "working with certain government entities on setting up such a mechanism."[18] Among the proposals has been direct capital injection by SAFE, effectively giving SAFE an equity stake in CIC. Another proposal would be for SAFE to entrust CIC to invest foreign exchange on its behalf – essentially an outsourcing relationship.[19] So far, however, no new arrangement has been made. In 2011, Chairman Lou Jiwei stated that he preferred more capital injections from MOF.[20] A potential explanation is that if SAFE were to directly inject capital, its equity stake in CIC would diminish MOF's managerial influence over CIC.

Lacking a stable funding mechanism, CIC has received only limited and erratic funding. SWFs in most countries manage the bulk of their country's foreign exchange; CIC's initial capitalization was $200 billion, accounting for just 15 percent of China's total reserves in 2007. Moreover, CIC has since received just one additional capital injection from the PBOC – a paltry $30 billion in December 2011. The sum was only confirmed in July 2012, after contradictory statements by CIC's leadership and false speculation in the media.* Many experts had expected CIC to receive an additional $100 billion a year.[21]

---

* CIC's second capital injection was a lengthy and chaotic process. In August 2009, Chairman Lou Jiwei stated that CIC might ask for more funds if its returns were solid and the country's currency reserves continued to rise. The reserves grew by $188 billion in the final four months of that year, ending 2009 at $2.4 trillion—$1 trillion more than the level than when CIC was established. In late 2009, Chinese media began to report that CIC was seeking $100 billion-$200 billion in additional funding. In March 2010, on the sidelines of the National People's Congress (NPC) annual meeting, CIC Executive Vice President Jesse Wang told reporters that CIC was short of cash and urged the National People's Congress to approve a plan to inject more capital. A week later, Yi Gang, the newly appointed head of SAFE, acknowledged for the first time that SAFE was studying this plan. But it was only a year later, in March 2011, during the next round of annual NPC meetings, that the central government's budget proposal included a bond program to inject funds into CIC, which was submitted to the NPC budget committee for review. In December 2011, an anonymous source told Reuters news agency that CIC was set to receive additional funding of $50 billion, which fueled media speculation in the ensuing months. However, CIC acknowledged in its annual report in July 2012 that it had received only $30 billion in additional capital, issued in December 2011. Dinny McMahon, "CIC Offers a Glimpse into U.S. Holdings," *Wall Street Journal* online, February 9, 2010, via Factiva; Reuters, "Exclusive: China's CIC to Get $50 Billion Boost,"December 23, 2011. http://www.reuters.com/article/2011/12/23/us-china-sovereign-idUSTRE7BM 09A20111223;Dow Jones International News, "China NPC: SAFE: Undecided on CIC Funding, to Grow Private Investment," March 8, 2010, via Factiva; Li Qing, "Fresh Capital En Route for Sovereign Fund CIC," *Caixin* online, May 17, 2011, via Factiva; *Jingji Cankao Bao,* "Rumors that CIC Has Already Been Approved for Capital Injection, Lou Jiwei Has Declined to Comment [Chuan Zhongtou yi huo Yanghang xin zhuzi Lou Jiwei wei yu zhiping]," February 14, 2012. http://news.xinhuanet.com/fortune/2012-02/14/c_122698414.htm; *and Simon Rabinovitch, "China Fund Loses 4.3% on Global Portfolio" Financial Times,* July 25, 2012, via Factiva.

**Table 2-1. CIC Capital Injections**

| Year | Amount ($ billions) |
|---|---|
| Sep 2007 | $200 |
| Dec 2011 | $30 |
| **Total** | **$230** |

Source: China Investment Corporation, *2011 Annual Report* (Beijing, China: July 2012).

What is more, CIC's funding has come in the form of debt instead of equity. For the initial capitalization of CIC, MOF issued special government bonds denominated in RMB that were purchased by China's commercial banks. The proceeds were then used to buy foreign exchange from the PBOC. For the PBOC, this was an expedient way to stabilize China's financial sector: The massive bond purchases effectively drained liquidity from bank balance sheets and stemmed inflation in much the same way as a bond issued by the PBOC in open market operations would do. For CIC, though, paying back the principal and interest on these bonds has been expensive.[22, *] It was reported that CIC and MOF agreed to classify the $200 billion capitalization as assets rather than debt in an effort to mitigate the debt burden on CIC. If this information is accurate, then MOF is now a partial shareholder in CIC entitled to dividend payments.[23, †] Yet this cosmetic change would have done little to ease the pressure on CIC to achieve high returns, and its second capital injection in 2011 was reported to again be in the form of debt.[24]

The competitive advantage of SWFs over other investors is arguably their ability to invest in the long term, since they are not accountable to individual shareholders. Owing to its funding arrangement, however, CIC has difficulty pursuing this model, because it needs to justify further funding and service its debts. Former CIC Chairman Lou stated soon after the founding of CIC that, based on the debt owed to MOF, the fund "needs to make RMB 300 million [US$46.6 million] on an average workday" to cover interest payments to MOF.[25] In its 2010 annual report, the fund claimed a shift in CIC's asset-

* The bonds in 2007 were issued in eight tranches at terms of ten years and 15 years, with interest ranging from 4.3 to 4.7 percent. CIC would have to repay this debt in RMB, even as the RMB further appreciated against the dollar, the currency in which CIC expected to earn its returns overseas.

† CIC reached the agreement with MOF in August 2009, according to an anonymous source from CIC in an interview with *China Economic Observer*. *China Economic Observer*. "CIC No Longer to Pay Interest to the State,", August 26, 2009. http://www. eeo.com.cn/ens/ homepage/briefs/2009/08/26/149395.shtml.

allocation strategy to reflect the growing importance of long-term investments and its decision to adopt a ten-year time horizon for its portfolio.[26]

### *CIC as a Domestic Investor*

CIC's ownership of domestic banking assets has also hampered its efforts to become a dedicated outbound investor. CIC took a vested interest in the solvency and profitability of the banks managed by Central Huijin, both to please the policymakers in Beijing as well as to maintain the value of its own assets. CIC was thus compelled to divert a large chunk of its capital to the domestic financial sector. About $100 billion of CIC's initial $200 billion in funding was transferred to domestic financial institutions through Central Huijin.[27, *]

Coupled with CIC's funding problems, the diversion of capital to the domestic banking sector has left the fund with very little capital to invest abroad. In 2009, the fund went on a spending spree that depleted its cash and deposits from $47.8 billion to $18.6 billion within one year. In 2010, cash and deposits sank further to $14.4 billion, and in 2011, increased only slightly to $20.1 billion.[†]

Furthermore, ownership of domestic bank shares has damaged CIC's credibility among foreign governments. That became especially evident at the Strategic and Economic Dialogue (S&ED) meetings between the United States and China in June 2008. At the meeting, U.S. negotiators put considerable pressure on China to clarify the domestic assets of its new SWF. The concern was that not only CIC, but also its banking subsidiaries – Industrial and Commercial Bank of China, Bank of China, and Agricultural Bank of China – were acquiring banking licenses to operate in the United States.[28]

Soon after the conclusion of the S&ED meetings, CIC decided to reorganize Central Huijin's board of directors to be independent of the CIC board.[29] At a meeting in late 2010, China's leadership also debated whether to split Central Huijin off from CIC. However, the proposal did not go through, apparently due to concerns that either the PBOC or MOF would fight to take over Central Huijin. Central Huijin's management also preferred to work under CIC, due to the benefits that come with an international institution with market and policy functions.[30]

---

[*] Huijin undertook a US$19 billion capital injection into Agriculture Bank of China Ltd., in preparation of its listing on the stock market. It also issued its own bonds worth $28 billion, which were bought by three domestic banks, and then used part of the proceeds to buy shares in those same banks, effectively inflating the banks' balance sheets.

[†] China Investment Corporation, *2011 Annual Report* (Beijing, China: July 2012), p.41.

Instead, CIC came to a piecemeal solution, formally splitting its domestic and foreign investment operations in December 2011. It created a new entity, CIC International, which served as an umbrella for CIC's outbound investment departments and overseas offices. Upon its establishment, CIC International was provided CIC's second capital injection of $30 billion in December 2011, "in a bid to enhance its role as a vehicle to diversify China's foreign exchange holdings."[31] The move was designed to reassure the outside world that CIC International was a separate investment entity that would not be affected by domestic considerations.

**Table 2-2. Comparison of Risk Appetite among Major Sovereign Wealth Funds**

| | Low Risk | | | | | | High Risk |
|---|---|---|---|---|---|---|---|
| **SWF** | **Cash/Gov. Bonds** | **Fixed Income** | **Equity** | **Real Estate** | **Hedge Funds** | **Private Equity** | **LBOs (Leveraged Buyouts)** |
| *Sovereign Stabilization Funds* | | | | | | | |
| Russian Reserve Fund | √ | | | | | | |
| *Sovereign Saving Funds* | | | | | | | |
| Timor Leste Petroleum Fund | √ | | | | | | |
| Norway Gov. Pension Fund | √ | √ | √ | | | | |
| Australian Future Fund | √ | √ | √ | | | | |
| GIC Singapore | √ | √ | √ | √ | √ | √ | |
| Qatar Investment Authority | √ | √ | √ | √ | √ | √ | |
| **China Investment Corporation** | √ | √ | √ | √ | √ | √ | |
| Abu Dhabi Investment Authority | √ | √ | √ | √ | √ | √ | |
| Kuwait Investment Authority | √ | √ | √ | √ | √ | √ | |
| Libyan Investment Authority | √ | √ | √ | √ | √ | √ | |
| *Government Investment Corporations* | | | | | | | |
| Vietnam Capital Investment Corp. | √ | √ | √ | √ | √ | √ | √ |
| Temasek Singapore | | | √ | √ | √ | √ | √ |

Source: Adapted from Eliot Kalter, "Sovereign Wealth Funds: Public Policy and Asset Allocation After the Financial Crisis" (Presentation at Fletcher Sovereign Wealth Fund Institute, Tufts Fletcher School, Medford, MA, October 2010). http://fletcher.tufts.edu/SWFI/~/media/151C34D306464CB38676207D0927306A.ashx.

These governance reforms have not, however, resolved the underlying problem of owning domestic assets. Contrary to claims of a "firewall" between domestic and international subsidiaries, CIC's chairman remains in charge of both CIC International and Central Huijin's boards. CIC also retains a vested interest in the profitability of China's state-owned banks to help increase the value of its balance sheet. Central Huijin, nominally barred from intervening in the banks' management, has continued to inject capital in them when necessary.[32]

## CIC's Commercial Investment Strategy

### *Asset Allocation*

SWFs assume varying levels of risk. On one end of the spectrum is the Russian Reserve Fund, which places nearly all its assets in fixed-income securities issued by foreign governments; on the other end is Temasek Singapore, which invests in assets that are less liquid and require high levels of capital upfront. CIC has considerable leeway to take risks within its mandate, which vaguely states that the fund should "diversify China's foreign exchange holdings and achieve higher long-term returns within acceptable risk tolerance."[33]

CIC took its first risks when it committed over $8 billion to buy equity in Wall Street firms Blackstone and Morgan Stanley in 2007. It made the investments just prior to the 2008 financial crisis, which resulted in major losses for the fund. CIC was not the only SWF to register substantial losses on Wall Street during the financial crisis; yet negative returns spread a reputation in China that CIC is a poor investor. For example, Ceng Gang, an economist at the Chinese Academy of Social Sciences Institute of Finance and Banking, a quasi-government think tank, has argued that CIC's initial Wall Street investments were "undeniably premature," because the fund had not had time to "analyze the current market situation and perfect their internal management."[34]

After retrenching in 2008, CIC received official backing in 2009 to resume its aggressive investment strategy.[*] CIC announced more than $8.15

[*] A 2009 editorial in the *People's Daily*, China's Communist Party-affiliated newspaper, reemphasized the role of CIC in diversifying China's foreign exchange reserves. Eiichi Sekine, "China's Foreign Exchange Reserves and China Investment Corporation's Steps towards Diversifying How It Manages Its Portion of Them," *Nomura Journal of Capital Markets* 1:4 (Winter 2009): 14.

billion of new acquisitions in 2009.[35] It began by acquiring more equities, which jumped from 3 percent to 43 percent of the portfolio within one year.[36] These included many small portfolio (<10 percent) stakes in publicly listed companies in the United States. CIC also made a series of equity investments beyond 10 percent in foreign companies, with a focus on energy and mining. Major investments included U.S. energy giant AES and Canadian mining company Teck Resources. At the end of 2011, when CIC was confident it would receive a second capital injection from the central bank, it resumed aggressive purchases of energy companies, including France's GDF Suez and Canada's Sunshine Oilsands.[37]

Further, CIC allocated more capital to alternative investments – a group of riskier asset classes comprising real estate, energy funds, hedge funds, and private equity. These jumped from 8 percent to 22 percent of the fund's financial assets in 2009-11. When CIC disclosed its investments in a filing to the Securities and Exchange Commission (SEC) in 2010, it revealed more than $1.5 billion of investments in 14 U.S.-based index funds. In April 2008, CIC also provided $4 billion to JC Flowers, a leading U.S. private equity firm, and upped its share in Blackstone.[38] CIC's hedge fund portfolio kicked off in 2009 with the appointments of Oaktree Capital Management, Capula Investment Management, and Blackrock to manage over $2 billion.[39,*]

CIC also entered real estate, considered by CIC's managers to be a safer bet than financial services and commodities.[40] In November 2010, it purchased a 7.6 percent interest in General Growth Properties Inc., a company with significant holdings in the U.S. real estate market. Just three months later, it joined AREA Real Estate Finance Corp to jointly acquire a preferred equity stake in a 27- story office building owned by Carlyle Group in Madison Avenue in Manhattan, home to the headquarters of Polo Ralph Lauren Corp.[41]

It is uncertain whether this higher-risk investment strategy is paying off. Due to the strong performance of its domestic holdings, CIC's cumulative returns have been fairly stable. And yet, the returns on its international

[*] To reflect this new investment strategy, CIC divided its "alternative investments" in 2011 into more concise categories. "Absolute returns" include primarily investments in hedge funds. "Long-term investments," in turn, comprise nonliquid direct investments in overseas companies, private equity, property and infrastructure, and commodities. CIC also reclassified its equities as "diversified public equities" in order to clarify that these were not long-term investments in companies overseas, but rather liquid shares in publicly listed companies. China Investment Corporation, *2011 Annual Report* (Beijing, China: July 2012), p.19.

portfolio have been volatile.* CIC registered double-digit gains on its outbound investments in 2009, 2010, and 2012, and negative returns in 2008 and 2011. In good years, CIC's management has not hesitated to highlight its competitive edge. In bad years, in turn, it has attributed poor performance to a "subdued global economic landscape" and noted that some other SWFs have taken similar risks.[42] Overall, the perception among many observers in China is that CIC is not yet a dependable investor.

### *Asset Management*

While struggling to find an optimal allocation for its assets, CIC has continually changed the way it manages its investments. CIC has outsourced 57 percent of its global investment portfolio and has made over 30 major transactions with external fund managers. CIC has adroitly leveraged its bargaining power in a market short of liquidity. It has not only entrusted money to outside managers but also has purchased equity in fund management firms, becoming a partial owner rather than just a client. CIC has also let funds compete against one another; in February 2010, it provided the $500 million in funding each to three different fund managers – Goldman Sachs, Lexington Partners, and Pantheon Ventures – and then discontinued its funding for Pantheon eight months later.[43]

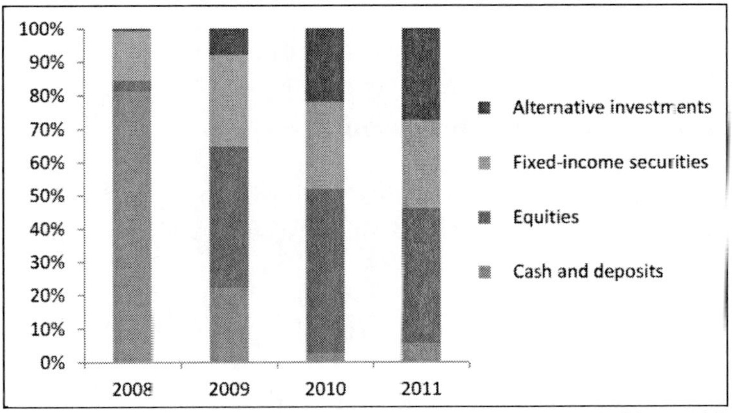


Source: China Investment Corporation, *2011 Annual Report* (Beijing, China: July 2012).

Figure 2-3. Breakdown of CIC's International Investments (Financial Assets).

---

* It is difficult to benchmark investment performance among SWFs, as the metrics used by different funds are not standardized, and some do not even publish annual returns.

Over time, CIC has made efforts to increase its in-house capacity as well. In 2008-11, the fund's staff nearly doubled from 194 to 376.[44] Among its high-level recruits was Gao Xiqing, the former manager of NSSF, China's other SWF, who was appointed in 2009 to head CIC's investment strategy. CIC also used the central government's Recruitment Program of Global Experts, also known as the "1000 plan," to target Chinese nationals working in the U.S. financial sector.[*]

A turning point came in February 2010, when Chairman Lou announced that CIC would increase the proportion of funds managed internally, because "our funds managed by external managers have not performed especially well."[45] In November of that year, CIC International (Hong Kong) Co., Ltd., CIC's first overseas subsidiary,[†] was established. CIC referred to the new entity as "a key platform for investment and financial trading activities such as fiduciary services and public listing of companies in which CIC has invested."[46] Just two months later, CIC opened a "representative office" in Toronto, with the goal of identifying promising investment opportunities in Canada's resource- rich economy.[47]

CIC's hiring push and the establishment of overseas offices have increased CIC's talent pool and ability to advise and manage its own investments. Internal management of its overseas portfolio moderately increased from 41 percent to 43 percent in 2011.[48] However, the majority of CIC's overseas portfolio remains under external management.

## Competition with Other Sovereign Investors

The founding of CIC did not prompt any precise rules as to what share of China's foreign exchange reserves the fund should receive or how it should

[*] An example is Fan Gongsheng, a PhD in mathematics from Columbia University, who worked in the U.S. banking sector for over 20 years. Dr. Fan was recruited to work at CIC under the "1000 plan" in 2008. He became director of CIC's fixed income and absolute return division in September that year. In November 2011, he was promoted to president of CIC's Hong Kong subsidiary, CIC International (Hong Kong) Co., Ltd. Baidu, http://baike.baidu.com/view/3707201.htm; Oriental Morning Post, "CIC's Hong Kong Subsidiary's Senior Executive Appointed [Zhongtou Xianggang Zigonsi Gaoguan Yi Daowei]," November 4, 2011. http://finance.eastmoney.com/news/1354,20111104174116378.html.

[†] CIC International (Hong Kong) Co., Ltd. is not to be confused with CIC Investment Corporation International Co., Ltd., CIC's branch responsible for managing overseas investment. For details, see CIC Organizational Structure (Figure A-3) in the Appendix.

coordinate its investments with other actors in China's economy. As a result, experts continue to dispute whether there is indeed a rivalry among Chinese investors to justify access to the PBOC's dollar reserves. Brad Setser of the Council on Foreign Relations argues that China's reserves are so large as to discourage competition.[49] Others argue that there is some division of labor in terms of the types of investments and the degree of risk assumed by different investors in China. The bulk of SAFE's reserves still consists of government bonds, cash, and other liquid assets, and it announced informal plans in 2013 to allocate only 5 percent of its reserves to riskier asset classes.[50] Similarly, NSSF's allocation of investment is more tightly controlled than CIC's, and any change in its mandate must be approved by the State Council.[51]

Judging by the past six years, however, competition among sovereign investors in China is intensifying nonetheless. As Patrick J. Schena, a scholar at the Sovereign Wealth Fund Institute at Tufts University, has noted:

> [...] with the formation of CIC, there appeared to exist grounds for a natural delegation of investment mandates: SAFE to invest China's overall foreign exchange reserve position; CIC to invest excess reserves. The evolving reality is far more nuanced. While the preponderance of China's reserves sit in U.S. government securities, SAFE has been nothing of an exclusively passive investor.[52]

Political scientists Sarah Eaton and Zhang Ming have even posited a "sovereign wealth fund tournament" by conscious design: "Although China's SWF tournament emerged as a quite unintended consequence of bureaucratic politics, China's leadership has since tacitly endorsed this rivalry because it has supplied the government with valuable carrot and stick mechanisms with which to discipline fund managers."[53]

**Table 2-3. SAFE Investments in the United Kingdom**

| Company/ property | Investment type | Date | Stake (%) | Investment ($ millions) |
|---|---|---|---|---|
| UPP Group Holdings | University housing | Jan-13 | 40% | 885 |
| Drapers Gardens | Office building | May-12 | 100% | 438 |
| Affinity Water | Water utility | Jun-12 | 10% | 186 |
| One Angel Square | Office building | Dec-12 | 49% | 107 |

Source: Adapted from Dinny McMahon and Wei Lingling, "China Quietly Invests Reserves in U.K. Properties," *Wall Street Journal*, February 24, 2013. http://online.wsj.com/article/SB10001424127887323699704578323670119279066.html.

CIC's main rival would appear to be SAFE's subsidiary SAFEIC. During the global financial crisis, it invested US$150 billion to $200 billion in U.S., European and Australian equities, including a 1.6 percent minority stake in oil and gas giant Total SA worth $2.8 billion.[54] After sustaining some losses during the crisis, SAFE disappeared from the radar for some time. In 2011, it recruited for multiple vacancies in Hong Kong to enhance its in-house asset-management capability. In early 2013, the *Wall Street Journal* reported that SAFE had used a third-party investor, Gingko Tree, to purchase real estate and utilities in the United Kingdom (UK) worth at least $1.6 billion.[55] SAFE also created a new Co-Financing Office in 2011 to make "innovative use" of China's reserves in order to "support financial institutions in serving China's economic growth and going-out strategy."[56]

NSSF is also emerging as a competitor. In late 2009, its Chairman Dai Xianglong announced that the fund had obtained permission to invest as much as 20 percent of its assets in overseas stocks and funds, 13 percent higher than the share until then. That would give NSSF the capacity to invest approximately $US30 billion to $40 billion overseas in a variety of assets.[57] These announcements coincided with CIC's renewed overseas acquisitions in late 2009. In April 2010, Chairman Dai projected that NSSF would more than double in size to $300 billion by 2015.[58]

**Table 2-4. China Development Bank: Assets, Disbursements, and Foreign Currency Loans**

| | 2005 | 2006 | 2007 | 2008 | 2009 | 2010 | 2011 | CAGR |
|---|---|---|---|---|---|---|---|---|
| Assets ($ billions) | 235.6 | 296.7 | 394.7 | 559.5 | 665.9 | 769.9 | 984.6 | 26.7% |
| Disbursements ($ billions) | 214.8 | 258.7 | 308.6 | 424.4 | 543.8 | 679.2 | 869.9 | 25.9% |
| FX loans ($ billions) | 16.2 | 28.7 | 30.5 | 64.5 | 82.7 | 141.3 | 187.3 | 54.2% |
| FX loans as share of total CDB loans | 7.5% | 11.1% | 9.9% | 15.2% | 15.2% | 20.8% | 21.5% | |
| FX loans as share of CDB loan growth | -- | 28.6% | 3.6% | 29.4% | 15.2% | 43.3% | 24.1% | |

Note: CAGR = Compound Annual Growth Rate; FX= Foreign Exchange Source: China Development Bank, 2005-2011 Annual Reports (Beijing, China). http://www.cdb.com.cn/english/Column.asp?ColumnId=91.

**Table 2-5. China's Sovereign Investors Working with Major Fund Managers**

| | | Chinese State-Sponsored Investor | | | | |
|---|---|---|---|---|---|---|
| | | **CIC** | **SAFE** | **NSSF** | **CICC** | **CDB** |
| **Firm** | TPG Capital (USA)[*] | | √ | | | √ |
| | Carlyle Group (USA)[†] | √ | √ | | √ | |
| | CDH Investments (Hong Kong)[‡] | | | √ | √ | |
| | Blackstone Group (USA)[§] | √ | √ | | | |

Source: See footnotes below.

In addition to SWFs, foreign exchange reserves are being distributed to state-owned banks. Of particular note is CDB, China's major policy bank. Set up in 1994, it is mandated to provide policy loans at below-market rates, as distinguished from commercial lending by commercial banks. However, the bank has exploited its sovereign credit rating and low capital adequacy ratios to pursue more profitable lending and has increasingly done so beyond

[*] *TPG Capital:* In 2008, SAFE invested US$2.5 billion in a TPG managed fund. CDB Capital, a wholly owned subsidiary of China Development Bank, purchased a minority stake in TPG in 2011, which established a cooperative partnership between the two firms. *Financial Times*, "China's Safe to Invest $2.5bn in TPG Fund," June 10, 2008. http://www. ft.com/ intl/cms/s/0/d793921e-3714-11dd-bc1c-0000779fd2ac.html#axzz2VFWfhCDu; People's Daily, "China Development Bank to Buy Stakes in U.S. Private Equity Fund," May 28, 2011. http://english.peopledaily.com.cn/90001/90778/90859/7393658.html.

[†] *Carlyle Group:* In 2010, CIC helped refinance a Manhattan, NY, office tower co-owned by Carlyle Group. In 2008, China International Capital Corporation (CICC) partnered with Carlyle to invest US$35 million in Shenzhen Aohua Medical Services Co. Ltd. SAFE is also reported to have planned to invest in funds managed by Carlyle. Bloomberg, "CIC Backs Carlyle's Manhattan Tower in U.S. Push," January 4, 2011. http://www. bloomberg.com/news/2011-01-03/cic-backs-manhattan-tower-as-china-steps-up-u-s-real-estate- investments.html; Asia *Private Equity Review*, "China's Institutional Investors are Buying Home Assets," February 1, 2009, via Factiva; *Greater China Private Equity Review Daily*, "China's SAFE Invests in Blackstone Real Estate Fund," July 27, 2012, via Factiva.

[‡] *CDH Investments:* In 2008, NSSF allocated RMB 2 billion US$288.1 million to a fund managed by CDH. In the same year, investment bank CICC teamed up with the firm to invest US$44 million in Hong Kong-listed South Beauty Catering Management Group. *Asia Private Equity Review*, "China's Institutional Investors are Buying Home Assets," February 1, 2009, via Factiva.

[§] *Blackstone Group:* In June 2009, CIC invested over US$500 million in a Blackstone hedge fund unit. In July 2012, SAFE committed $500 million to a Blackstone property fund as part of its plan to allocate 5 percent of reserves in alternative investments. Bloomberg, "CIC Said to Invest $500 Million in Hedge Funds, Blackstone," June 19, 2009. http://www.bloomberg.com/apps/news?pid=newsarchive&sid=aEyh5EUNjlbo; Wall Street Journal, "China Invests $500 Million in Blackstone Fund," July 26, 2012. http://online.wsj com/article/SB10000872396390443477104577550574246215012.html.

China's borders. CDB's foreign exchange loans in 2005-11 grew at twice the rate of the bank's overall loans and increased their share of total loans from 7.5 percent to 21.5 percent. CDB has played a central role in the government's "go global" strategy to fund Chinese companies investing abroad.

Like CIC, these other state-sponsored investors are working closely with international fund managers. In 2008, SAFEIC led the way with a $2.5 billion investment in a fund run by U.S. private- equity firm TPG, which joined the buyout firm in taking a stake in Washington Mutual, Inc.[59] SAFEIC also committed $500 million to a real estate private-equity fund managed by Blackstone Group LP.[60] NSSF, for its part, received permission in June 2008 to invest up to 10 percent of its portfolio in China's domestic private equity funds.[61] As a result, it became a pioneer for investing in this nascent industry. In July 2012, NSSF announced that it had signed agreements with 12 global investment managers.[62] Two months later, the *Wall Street Journal* passed on a rumor that NSSF was also considering investing in foreign private-equity funds.[63],[*] CDB, in turn, has purchased minority stakes in European banks Barclay's and ABN Amro. In May 2011, it joined two foreign SWFs, Singapore's GIC and the Kuwait Investment Authority, to buy a 4.5 percent stake in TPG, marking its entry into the private equity space.

## SECTION 3: CIC AS A STRATEGIC INVESTOR

As state-sponsored entities, SWFs are answerable to governments rather than private individuals. The inherent risk is that SWFs will pursue noncommercial objectives to further the strategic interests of their sponsoring government. When USCC Commissioners met with Gao Xiqing, CIC's president, in the spring of 2008, Mr. Gao stated unequivocally that CIC is operating on a commercial basis.[64] As this section demonstrates, however, CIC has also pursued strategic objectives as part of China's "go global" policy.

---

[*] China's burgeoning private equity market has attracted U.S. firms, such as Blackstone, Carlyle Group, and TPG, looking to shift capital from the recessionary markets in the United States and Europe to emerging markets. In December 2011, the NDRC issued the first nationwide regulations governing private equity and venture capital funds, helping U.S. firms to enter this market ," *Asia Private Equity Review*, "China's Institutional Investors Are Buying Home Assets," February 1, 2009, via Factiva.

## Coordinated Investment in Strategic Sectors

CIC has made strategic investments both upstream, in resources, and downstream, in utilities and logistics. These investments are targeted at areas in which China's economy has structural weaknesses. Most of these transactions occurred in 2009, when CIC had very strong cash flow and focused its investments on commodities. In many cases, there is evidence of coordination with other Chinese enterprises.

### *Oil and Gas*

On the upstream side, CIC has aimed to mitigate China's growing dependence on resource imports. One example is the oil and gas sector. China imports about three-fifths of its oil, and at the end of 2012 overtook the United States as the world's leading (net) importer.[65] China is now importing more oil at a higher per-unit cost, placing a serious strain on Chinese industries dependent on petrochemicals. One countermeasure by the government has been to encourage China's national oil companies to boost equity oil production overseas in order to reduce exposure to price volatility and to profit from improved terms of trade.[66]

In September 2009, CIC took a 45 percent interest in Russia's state-owned Nobel Oil Group. Although the shares purchased were worth only $100 million, CIC paid an additional $150 million to acquire and develop Nobel's oilfields in Russia. Two Chinese firms based in Hong Kong – Oriental Patron Financial Group and Kaishun Energy – joined CIC and bought shares in Nobel to bring the Chinese stake to 50 percent.[67] This investment took place just seven months after China National Petroleum Corporation (CNPC), one of China's oil majors, extended a long-term, $25 billion loan to Russia in exchange for 300 million tons of oil piped from Russia's largest oil producer.[68]

CIC has also played a strategic role in the natural gas sector. Gas is not only a cleaner alternative to oil but has also become more cost competitive and transportable, thanks to technological advances in liquefaction and fracking. Although China's demand for natural gas is expected to double in 2009- 15, China currently holds just 1.5 percent of the world's proven reserves.[69]

In September 2009, CIC purchased an 11 percent stake in JSC KazMunaiGas Exploration Production, the largest natural gas producer in neighboring Kazakhstan.[70] The deal was relevant when considering China's expanding energy partnership with Kazakhstan. CNPC is a part owner of five Kazakh oilfields, two exploration projects, and multiple pipelines. The Kazakh-China Oil Pipeline was a joint investment between CNPC and

KazMunaiGas that became operational in July 2006. CNPC has also purchased a stake in another Kazakh gas company, Mangistai Munai Gas.[71] In April 2009, CNPC and China-Exim Bank lent a combined $10 billion to secure oil and gas assets in Kazahkstan, very similar to China's deal with Russia.[72]

CIC subsequently set its sights on prominent gas companies in the United States. In 2010, it invested $200 million in Chesapeake Energy, the U.S.'s second-largest gas producer. Soon afterward, China's oil majors China National Offshore Oil Corporation (CNOOC) and China Petroleum and Chemical Corporation (Sinopec) made multibillion-dollar investments in gas fields operated by Chesapeake in Texas, Colorado, and Oklahoma.[73]

In August 2012, CIC contributed $500 million to construct an LNG production and export terminal in Louisiana, run by a subsidiary of the U.S. firm Cheniere Energy.[74] Four months later, Cheniere entered into a sales agreement with the North American subsidiary of Total SA, a French multinational oil and gas giant, to ship oil from the Louisiana terminal to Asia. It is worth noting that Chinese SWF SAFEIC purchased a 1.6 percent stake in Total back in 2008.[75] Total proceeded to sign LNG supply contracts with China's national oil companies, CNOOC, Petrochina, and Sinopec, and by 2012, accounted for one-tenth of China's LNG imports.[76]

Outside the United States, CIC's largest investment in the gas sector was a $4.2 billion, 30 percent interest in the exploration and production subsidiary of France's GDF Suez. The August 2011 deal included a 10 percent stake in a liquefaction facility operated by Atlantic LNG, one of the world's largest LNG producers. The two parties also launched a long-term strategic partnership. Like Total SA, GDF Suez is becoming a key LNG supplier to China's leading oil and gas companies. Just three months after initiating its partnership with CIC, GDF Suez was contracted to sell 2.6 million tons annually to CNOOC, starting from 2013. According to the agreement, GDF Suez will also provide CNOOC with a floating storage and regasification unit. This sequence of deals suggests that CIC is helping finance LNG production by GDF Suez, and this production in turn is sold to CNOOC.[77]

### *Mining*

Another example of CIC's strategic investment is the mining sector. While China has major reserves of iron ore, these are of poor quality and hard to access. Propelled by a booming steel industry, China by 2008 accounted for three-fifths of world iron ore imports.[78] A major concern is bargaining leverage, because hundreds of steel mills in China buy iron ore, while an oligopoly of three companies – Vale do Rio Doce, Rio Tinto, and BHP

Billiton – accounts for 60 percent of the global iron ore trade.[*] In other important metals, like copper and bauxite, China also depends on imports from a select few large mining companies.

More recently, CIC has also become a net importer of coal. Although China is the world leader in coal production and reserves, coal accounts for two-thirds of the country's energy consumption, and demand is concentrated in China's coastal regions, far from the coal mining sites further inland. Rail infrastructure suitable for transporting coal is underdeveloped, making it difficult and costly to transport domestically extracted coal to coastal cities. That makes it attractive to import coal via China's large, modern seaports.[79]

Growing reliance on imports has prompted Chinese producers to invest in mining assets overseas, and CIC has joined in these efforts. In July 2009, the fund spent $1.5 billion to become the top shareholder of Teck Resources, Canada's largest independent mining company. Teck's major products include copper, steelmaking coal (coke), and zinc, and it relies on business with China for a quarter of its total revenue.[80] Teck has been eager to expand its business in China following the investment, and in its 2009 annual report stated that "China is an important market for our businesses and we look forward to the opportunity to work with [CIC] to strengthen our position in that market for our mutual benefit." CIC's investment has allowed Teck to advance business with Chinese companies such as Jiangxi Copper Co., China's largest integrated copper producer, which was reported to be one of Teck's largest clients, importing over 60,000 tons of copper ore concentrates from Teck's copper mine in Chile.[81] Teck has also recently established an office in Shanghai to further strengthen business ties in China.[82]

Further, the Teck acquisition laid the groundwork for CIC's inroads into Canada, as the fund established its first overseas representative office in Toronto soon afterward. Marcia Smith, a Teck vice president, stated that CIC's investment in Teck would bring the companies mutual deal opportunities.[83] Just months after the Teck acquisition, CIC bought a $500 million, 13 percent stake in another Canadian firm, SouthGobi Resources Ltd., which specializes in coal production and development in Mongolia, from where coal products are shipped across the border into China.[84]

In the fall of 2009, CIC extended a six-year, $1.9 billion loan to Indonesia's largest coal producer, PT Bumi Resources. Indonesia is China's largest coal supplier in the Asia-Pacific region.[85] The loan was aimed not only

[*] For a detailed study, see Regina M. Abrami and Iacob Koch-Weser. "Heavy Metal (A): Baosteel Enters Brazil," Harvard Business School Case 912-411, May 2012. (Revised from original December 2011 version.)

at capital investments to expand Bumi's mining infrastructure but also at helping Bumi to service its debt during a market downturn. [86] In 2012, PT Bumi posted a net loss of $666 million due to a drop in coal prices and threatened to default on its debt payments to both CIC and several foreign banks, including J.P. Morgan and Bank of America Merrill Lynch. [87] One of the creditors that helped the Indonesian firm refinance its debt was CDB, the Chinese policy bank, which provided a $600 million loan.[88] Given its part ownership of CDB, CIC may have contributed indirectly to the bailout of PT Bumi.

In Australia, CIC also came close to negotiating a politically sensitive mining deal. The fund reportedly joined Chinese state-owned mining company Shenhua Energy in 2009 to negotiate a $3 billion equity investment in Fortescue, Australia's third-largest iron miner. Hunan Valin, a provincial steel producer in China, owns a 17.5 percent stake in Fortescue, and Shanghai Baosteel, China's largest steel producer, also operates a joint venture with the firm. Although the negotiations did not materialize, CIC's intention was in all likelihood strategic.[89] The negotiations came on the heels of a failed share acquisition of Rio Tinto, Fortescue's larger Australian competitor, by a Chinese steel company. Rio Tinto's China office chief Stern Hu was also arrested at the time on allegations of espionage.[90]

CIC has engaged as well with foreign financial institutions to acquire equity in mining producers. In December 2011, it bought a 25 percent interest in Shanduka Group, a South African investment holdings company that owns and controls businesses in the resource sector. CIC was granted representation in the Shanduka management and currently has two seats on Shanduka's board of directors. Following CIC's investment, Shanduka Group undertook sizable resource transactions, including the acquisition of a controlling stake in Shanduka Coal, which owns numerous coal mines located throughout South Africa.[91]

### *Utilities and Logistics*

A final example of strategic investment is in logistics and utilities, downstream industries that are indirectly related to energy and resources.

China's utilities are in the process of upgrading power generation and distribution capacity in order to generate power more cleanly, efficiently, and farther from urban centers. Notably, the United States has been supportive of China in these efforts. In 2009, Duke Energy, the largest power company in the United States, began cooperating with Huaneng Group, one of China's "Big Five" utilities, to develop clean energy technologies.[92] China has also become the world leader in installed wind power capacity, although many wind farms are not properly connected to the power grid.*

In November 2009, CIC invested $1.6 billion for a 15 percent stake in U.S. utility company AES Corporation. CIC was keen on joining a global company such as AES, which has an installed power capacity over 40,000 megawatts (MW) and over 132 power generation facilities in 29 countries.[93] AES also has a lengthy track record in the Chinese energy market. AES set up its Chinese subsidiary in 1994; Paul Hanrahan, the AES chief executive officer in 2009, had run the Chinese unit when it was first established. By 2009, AES had seven operating facilities in China.

AES' power-generating capacity in China is moderate, accounting for just over 6 percent of AES' global installed power capacity in 2010.[94] Of greater interest to CIC at the time of the acquisition was AES' leading role in China's clean energy sector. In the early 2000s, the U.S. firm shifted from operating fossil fuel power plants in China to developing wind farms, effectively becoming an intermediary between Chinese turbine makers and Chinese utility companies. Sinovel, China's second-largest wind turbine maker, became AES' supplier of choice, ahead of foreign manufacturers like General Electric and Vestas.[95] Under its initial agreement with CIC, AES was going to sell the SWF an additional 35 percent stake in its wind-generation business.[96] AES at the time had 1,200 MW of new wind projects that would require $600 million in equity over 18 months. AES was hoping to use some of this capital in order to finance exports of Chinese-made turbines for its wind farms in Vietnam.[97]

CIC ultimately opted not to purchase the stake in the AES wind power business. And yet, it did help AES find other Chinese partners. In February 2012, State Grid Corp., China's largest utility company, took an 80 percent stake in the AES wind power business. The investment formed part of State Grid's foray into international markets, including the acquisition of power grids in Brazil and a privatized utility company in Portugal.[98]

In logistics, CIC has made two notable investments. In September 2009, it purchased an $850 million, 14.9 percent stake in Noble Group Ltd., a Hong Kong-based global supply chain manager of agricultural, industrial, and energy products. Noble holds about $300 billion worth of assets and is one of the main companies shipping commodities, such as soybeans, from Latin America to China. In 2011, CIC also began to partner with Global Logistic Properties Limited (GLP), a company that owns and leases modern logistics

* For details, see Regina M. Abrami and Iacob Koch-Weser, "Goldwind USA: Chinese Wind in the Americas." Harvard Business School Case 912-416, May 2012.

facilities across China and Japan. In November 2012, CIC participated in GLP's expansion into logistics facilities in Brazil, the premier commodity exporter to China in the Latin America region. CIC did so by acquiring a $460 million, 34.2 percent stake in a joint venture alongside Canada Pension Plan Investment Board and Government Investment Corp., one of Singapore's SWFs.[99]

## CIC as an Active Investor

Besides the allocation and coordination of investment, CIC has also been strategic in its choice of governance models. SWFs tend to act as silent partners who put up capital but have little influence on execution, terms, or future strategy. Few SWFs have the infrastructure and inclination to actively participate in the management of businesses.[100] In response to concerns about CIC taking controlling stakes in its investments, CIC President Gao told USCC Commissioners in 2008 that the fund does not want board seats and has instructions to take passive roles in its investments.[101]

**Table 3-1. CIC Affiliated Positions in Management**

| Company | CIC stake | Country | Board member | Position | Year appointed |
|---|---|---|---|---|---|
| Teck Resources | 17.2% | Canada | Felix Chee, Special Advisor | Adviser to CIC's chief investment officer | 2010 |
| AES | 15.0% | USA | Zhang Guobao, Director | Vice chairman of the Chinese National Development and Reform Commission and recently held the position of administrator (Minister- level) of the Chinese National Energy Administration | 2011 |
| Shanduka Group | 25.1% | South Africa | Wang Hui, Nonexecutive Director | Director of the Head of the Metals and Mining Team of the Special Investments Department of CIC | 2012 |
| | | | Hu Bing, Nonexecutive Director | Managing director, head of Special Investments Department of CIC | |
| Heathrow Ltd. | 10.0% | Britain | Zhang Qing (King), Nonexecutive Director | Managing director of the Special Investments Department at CIC | 2013 |

Sources: Teck Resource, AES, Shanduka Group, Heathrow Ltd.

However, CIC has gained influence on the boards of four companies in which it has acquired a stake of 10 percent or more. In 2010, Felix Chee, an adviser to CIC's chief investment officer, was appointed to the board of Teck Resources. Mr. Chee is a Canadian of Chinese descent who spent most of his career in Canada's financial services industry. He helped put the Teck deal together, and around the time of joining Teck's board, he was busy establishing CIC's first overseas representative office in Toronto.[102]

In December 2011, CIC was also granted the right to appoint one member to the board of AES. The person chosen was not from within CIC; rather, it was a high-level Chinese government official, Zhang Guobao, who served as vice chairman of the NDRC, China's premier planning agency. Before joining NDRC, Mr. Zhang had held the position of administrator of the Chinese National Energy Administration, a powerful new body in charge of energy policy.[103]

## Cooperation with Other SWFs

CIC has participated in China's economic diplomacy through cooperation with other SWFs. Two notable examples are Singapore and Russia.

CIC officials have indicated that Singapore's SWFs have served as models for their own fund. Moreover, China International Capital Corporation (CICC), one of China's largest investment banking and research services companies, founded in 1995, counts Singapore's SWF GIC among its shareholders.[104] Temasek, the Singaporean SWF, has also purchased the Hong Kong-listed shares of China's major commercial banks – the same banks in which Central Huijin is the major shareholder.[105]

Further, in several cases, CIC and Singapore's SWFs have transacted with the same companies overseas. One example is the U.S. gas sector, where CIC invested in Chesapeake Energy and Cheniere Energy alongside Singapore's SWFs. Chesapeake issued $900 million in convertible preferred stock, which was purchased by CIC, Korea Investment Corporation, and Singapore's Temasek.[106] Like CIC, Singapore's GIC contributed $500 million to the construction of Cheniere's new LNG production and export platform in Louisiana. Prior to this, Cheniere had attracted investment from Temasek as well.[107] In the logistics sector, GIC joined CIC in supporting the expansion of Global Logistics Properties into Latin America.[108]

In contrast to Singapore, CIC's cooperation with Russia is explicit and carries stronger political overtones. In the wake of the global financial crisis, many foreign investors left Russia, and global gas prices fell, putting immense pressure on Russia's balance of payments. In September 2010, Russian Finance Minister Alexei Kudrin announced that the government was preparing to sell $10 billion worth of state-owned assets per year for approximately five years. Nine months later, Moscow founded the Russian Direct Investment Fund (RDIF), a private equity vehicle under Russia's state-owned bank Vnesheconombank (VEB). RDIF's principal aim is to counteract the sharp drop in Russia's FDI inflows by courting foreign investors, both sovereign and private. RDIF is mandated to secure co-investment that as a minimum matches Russia's own commitment.[109]

CIC became the first foreign investor to commit to RDIF, doing so through the creation of a Russia- China Investment Fund (RCIF). RCIF effectively became a subsidiary of RDIF, taking the form of a limited partnership. The initial agreement was made in October 2011 during a visit by Russian Prime Minister Vladimir Putin to Beijing and was officially launched at a signing ceremony in Beijing in June 2012. The Russians matched CIC's contribution of $1 billion.[110]

It is questionable whether CIC's investment in RCIF was only commercially motivated. The deal came just after Presidents Hu and Putin had failed to conclude sensitive talks about planned gas pipelines before President Hu's state visit to Moscow in June 2012, owing to price disputes between Russia's OAO Gazprom and CNPC. Some analysts argue that the deal serves as a way to diversify Russia and China's bilateral investment beyond the oil and gas sectors. RCIF's stated focus is on higher value-added industries like engineering, agriculture, commodity processing, and transport infrastructure in Russia, which would use Chinese technology and contractors.[111]

The strategic role of CIC in Sino-Russian diplomacy was further evidenced in February 2013, when CIC invested in the initial public offering (IPO) of the Moscow Exchange. The IPO raised $499 million, including $80 million from RDIF and a further $200 million from other direct investors. According to one source, CIC at least matched the RDIF investment.[112] This transaction appears to have had little commercial value for CIC, which has avoided equity investments in financial services companies since 2010.

## Financial Support for Chinese Enterprises

A final form of strategic behavior has been CIC's direct financial support for Chinese enterprises. One way in which the fund has done this is through its domestic subsidiary Central Huijin. As discussed in Section 2, CIC acts as a shareholder of China's largest financial institutions, and these in turn are the creditors of major Chinese enterprises. Central Huijin has also circumvented the banks it owns to provide capital directly to enterprises.* For example, it has taken a majority stake in China Reinsurance (Group) Corporation and a minority interest in the Internet service company Alibaba.[113]

A second form of support for Chinese enterprises is through CIC's other subsidiary, CIC International. It has taken equity stakes in Chinese firms listed in Hong Kong and other international exchanges. Share purchases include $100 million in China Railway Group (2007); $400 million in Longyuan Power Group (2009); $710 million in GCL Poly (Hong Kong) Energy Ltd. (2009); $816 million in Changsha Heavy Industry (2010); and $250 million in Semiconductor Manufacturing International Corporation (SMIC) (2011).[114] The firms are generally state-owned and belong to China's pillar industries – transport logistics, heavy industry, and power generation. Issuing public shares has been a common strategy for these firms to raise capital, but investors often lack confidence in the profitability of recently restructured SOEs. In the wake of the global financial crisis, the stock market has also been lackluster. Presumably, CIC purchased shares in order to buoy the companies' share prices.

The investment in GCL-Poly Hong Kong suggests more strategic motives. Poly-Hong Kong is the subsidiary of China Poly Group Corp., a business group that operates in dozens of industries in China. According to a groundbreaking report by Bloomberg published in 2012, the group is operated by the son of a Chinese revolutionary general and has close links to other members of the leadership.† In 2009, CIC became the second-largest shareholder of GCL Poly (Hong Kong) Energy Ltd., China's largest producer of polysilicon, a chemical material that is used for solar panels and other industrial applications. The two sides also agreed to set up an additional joint

* According to a 2005 estimate, 70 percent of new loans originating from state-owned banks in China are granted to state-owned enterprises. Michael F. Martin, "China's Banking System: Issues for Congress" (Washington, DC: Congressional Research Service February 10, 2012), p.40. http://www.fas.org/sgp/crs/row/R42380.pdf.

† According to Bloomberg, GCL Poly was founded by Wang Jun, the son of a famous Chinese general. The company initially sold weapons to Iran, Burma, and Pakistan in the 1980s and then expanded into various other industries, including coal mines, real estate, movie theaters, and travel televisions. As Bloomberg has shown, relatives of China's Eight Immortal revolutionaries have an interest in the company. Bloomberg. "Heirs of Mao's Comrades Rise as New Capitalist Nobility," December 26, 2012. http://www.bloomberg.com/news/2012-12-26/immortals-beget-china-capitalism-from-citic-to-godfather-of-golf.html.

venture company with registered capital of $500 million to invest in solar power projects, in which GCL would own the 51 percent majority stake.[115] Further, also in 2009, CIC purchased a $53 million, 2.3 percent stake in Poly (Hong Kong) Investments Ltd., the offshore property flagship of Poly Group. At the time of the CIC acquisition, Poly-Hong Kong owned some 9.4 million square meters of real estate in over a dozen Chinese cities.[116]

# SECTION 4: CIC GOVERNANCE

## Enhanced Transparency and Accountability

Since the USCC held its hearing on China's SWFs in 2008, international regulation and monitoring of SWFs has improved in many areas. The International Working Group of Sovereign Wealth Funds (IWG), established by the International Monetary Fund, has set out Generally Accepted Principles and Practices (GAPP), commonly referred to as the "Santiago Principles." The Santiago Principles' stated aim is to "promote a clearer understanding of the institutional framework, governance, and investment operations of SWFs in order to facilitate free-flowing international investment."[117,*] SWFs sign on to the principles voluntarily. Their compliance is monitored, albeit not subject to any hard enforcement.

The Santiago Principles have also spawned corollary efforts to make SWFs more accountable. The Sovereign Wealth Fund Initiative, headquartered at Tufts University in Boston, conducts research and convenes managers of SWFs with policymakers and businesses. The IMF's International Forum of Sovereign Wealth Funds (IFSWF) meets at least once a year to exchange views on issues of common interest to SWFs and to facilitate an understanding of the Santiago Principles. In addition, private institutes have published their own assessments of SWF governance. Edwin M. Truman, senior fellow at the Peterson Institute for International Economics in Washington, DC, developed the so-called Truman Scoreboard, an independent, periodic assessment of SWFs based on quantifiable metrics.[118] A similar rating method, the Linaburg-

* The principles are divided into three pillars: (i) Legal Framework, Objectives, and Macroeconomic Linkages (Principles 1-5); (ii) Institutional Framework and Governance Structure (Principles 6-17); (iii) Investment and Risk Management Framework (Principles 18-24).

Maduell Transparency Index (LMTI), was developed by the Sovereign Wealth Fund Institute (SWFI).*

Initially, CIC was reluctant to increase transparency. In an interview with CBS Television's *60 Minutes* in early 2008, CIC President Gao Xiqing pledged that CIC is "going to do things" to be as open as Norway's SWF, considered to be one of the world's most transparent; yet he stated that the Santiago Principles "will only hurt feelings" and are neither economically nor politically useful.[119] CIC was not alone in its reluctance to become more transparent – as wealthy economies suffered during the global financial crisis, many SWFs, especially those in the Gulf States, felt they had significant leverage to resist tighter regulation and still obtain market access.[120]

However, CIC eventually shifted course, going so far as to participate in the drafting of the Santiago Principles in September 2008. The Chinese government officially endorsed the principles upon their promulgation by the IWG in October that year.[121] A possible explanation for this change in attitude is that leading SWFs, including in Norway and Singapore, agreed to higher transparency standards first, placing pressure on CIC to do the same.† China became even more proactive in 2011, hosting the third meeting of the IFSWF, at which China's then Vice Premier Li Keqiang spoke. The forum resulted in the Beijing Declaration, by which SWFs agreed to establish a permanent secretariat in the IMF to oversee the regulation of SWFs and their commitments under the Santiago Principles. Jin Liqun, who served as chairman of CIC's board of supervisors until March 2013, was elected to chair the IFSWF.[122]

* The Linaburg-Maduell Transparency Index is based on ten essential principles that depict sovereign wealth fund transparency to the public. The index ranges from 1 to 10, with 10 being the most transparent. The principles used to assess the SWFs include information about creation, origins of wealth, and government ownership structure; audited annual reports; ownership percentage of company holdings; total portfolio value; clear strategies and objectives; information about subsidiaries and external managers; and ethical standards. http://www.swfinstitute.org/statistics-research/linaburg-maduell-transparency-index/.

† According to Ted Truman of the Peterson Institute, the GAPP negotiations made progress because countries with SWFs were a fragmented interest group, constituting a mix of developing, middle-income, and advanced countries. Daniel W. Drezner, a noted China expert, has argued that, while countries with SWFs formed a fragmented interest group, advanced economies who received their investments shared common interests, and were thus able to demand tougher rules under the aegis of the IMF. The Sovereign Wealth Fund Initiative, "A Conversation with Ted Truman, Senior Fellow, Peterson Institute for International Economics," March 2012; Daniel W. Drezner, "Bad Debts: Assessing China's Financial Influence in Great Power Politics," International Security 34:2 (Fall 2009): 28-31.

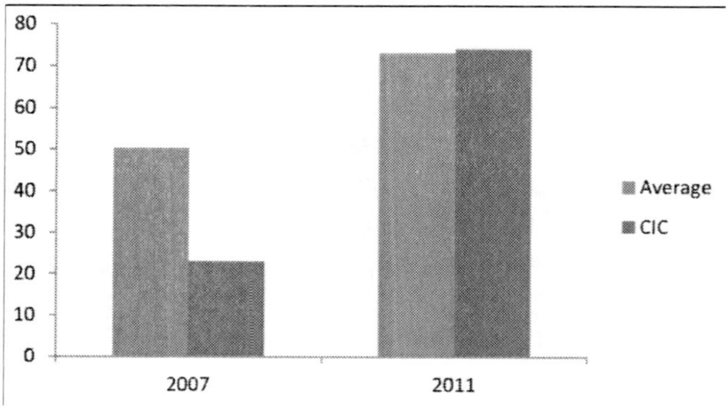


Note: Final scores given to individual SWFs range from 0-100, with 100 representing full compliance.

Sources: Sarah Bagnall and Edwin M. Truman, *IFSWF Report on Compliance with the Santiago Principles: Admirable but Flawed Transparency* (Washington, DC: Peterson Institute for International Economics, August 2011), p. 2; Edwin M. Truman, *Sovereign Wealth Funds: Is Asia Different?* (Washington, DC: Peterson Institute for International Economics, June 2011), p. 24.

Figure 4-1. Truman Scores, 2011.

In terms of compliance, CIC has not been outstanding but has certainly outperformed many other SWFs, particularly in the Gulf States. CIC published its first annual report in July 2009 and has since provided significant detail on its holdings and financial accounts, including annual returns on its outbound portfolio. In contrast, Singapore's GIC only began to report five-year and ten-year annualized returns in July 2011.[123] Moreover, CIC has scored fairly well in independent surveys: it ranks twenty-third among 48 SWFs surveyed in the SWFI's latest LMTI score and eleventh out of 34 SWFs on the Truman Scoreboard.

In July 2009, the same month that it published its first annual report, CIC also held the inaugural meeting of its International Advisory Council.[124] The Council was modeled after similar bodies at SWFs in Singapore and Norway. In CIC's case, it is composed of 15 advisors and one secretariat. It has four U.S. advisors:

- *Merit E. Janow.* Professor of International Economic Law and International Affairs, Columbia University; Chairman, NASDAQ Stock Market LLC; former member of the Appellate Body of the WTO.

- *John L. Thornton*. Professor and director of Global Leadership at Tsinghua University in Beijing; Chairman of the board of trustees at The Brookings Institution; Co-chairman, Barrick Gold Corporation; Nonexecutive chairman of HSBC North America; former president of Goldman Sachs Group.
- *James D. Wolfensohn*. – Chairman of Wolfensohn & Company; former president of the World Bank Group; former chairman of the Citigroup International Advisory Board.
- *John J. Mack*. Chairman emeritus, former chief executive officer of Morgan Stanley.*

## Problems with CIC's Governance

### *Personnel and Organization*

Although CIC has made efforts to improve transparency, an underlying concern remains its close relationship with the Chinese government. SWFs are generally quasi-independent entities with low levels of government interference. It is not uncommon for government officials to retain board representation, but their presence is usually balanced by professionals who are hired on a meritocratic basis.[125]

CIC, in contrast, maintains very close ties to the state. Of the 25 individuals staffing CIC's board of supervisors, board of directors, and executive committee, only three individuals are not current or former government officials: Vice President Wang Jianxi, who spent many years on Wall Street; Chief Strategy Officer Zhou Yuan, the former vice chair of the Hong Kong Mercantile Exchange; and Chief Information Technology Officer Hua Hua, who was the former vice president of Great Wall Software International Ltd., a government-sponsored information technology (IT) firm.[126]

CIC's mandate requires that five government agencies be represented on its board. One of the agencies represented is the NDRC, a superministry in charge of industrial planning that has little to do with monetary policy. In 2007-12, an NDRC official served as nonexecutive director, while a former

* Remaining international advisors are Zeng Peiyan (China), Shaukat Aziz (Pakistan), Frederick Ma (Hong Kong, China), Taizo Nishimuro (Japan), Yingyi Qian (China), Andrew Sheng (Malaysia), Joseph Yan (Hong Kong, China), Omari Issa (Tanzania), Knut N. Kjaer (Norway), Jean Lemierre (France), and Lord Nicholas H. Stern (United Kingdom). China Investment Corporation, *2011 Annual Report* (Beijing, China: July 2012), p.17.

NDRC official was chief risk officer. Moreover, in 2009, CIC appointed Li Keping, the head of China's social security fund, NSSF, to become CIC's chief investment officer. Mr. Li's success at NSSF may have merited the appointment, yet it further deepened CIC's ties to the state.[127] Also on CIC's board are former heads of the Bank of Communications, China Construction Bank, and the Export- Import Bank. Through its subsidiary Central Huijin, CIC owns equity in all of these financial institutions. [128]

Furthermore, the leadership transitions at CIC suggest a "revolving door" among top government agencies. It is common practice at SWFs to allow top managers to stay on for many years in order to provide continuity and to oversee investments with long time horizons.[129] That does not appear to be the case at CIC, which in 2013 became enmeshed in China's once-in-a-decade leadership transition. CIC Chairman Lou was appointed Minister of Finance, essentially returning to his former employer, where he had served as vice minister until 2007. As yet, no successor has been named to head the fund. CIC is an anomaly, as Beijing's other top finance jobs – head of the central bank, China Development Bank, and the four largest commercial banks –were all filled.[130]

In April 2013, Tu Guangshao, the former vice mayor of Shanghai and veteran financial services regulator at the PBOC and the CSRC, was reported to become Chairman Lou's successor. It was later revealed that he was not interested in the post. Yi Gang, deputy governor at the PBOC, also declined an offer for the chairmanship.[131] Eyes have turned to CIC Vice Chairman and President Gao Xiqing, who has temporarily taken leadership of CIC in Chairman Lou's absence. Although qualified, Mr. Gao is not being considered because he is a Wall Street veteran who lacks Communist Party credentials, according to sources familiar with the situation.[132]

Despite the uncertainty of who will become chairman, CIC did fill its other leadership post on the supervisory board. CIC Supervisory Board Chairman Jin Liqun left to became the head of China International Capital Corp., a quasi-government investment bank majority owned by CIC's subsidiary Central Huijin. Taking Mr. Jin's place at CIC was Li Xiaopeng, the vice head of the Industrial and Commercial Bank of China (ICBC).[*] ICBC is one of the commercial banks owned by Central Huijin.

Furthermore, CIC is required under China's Company Law to have a Communist Party committee. However, no mention is made of this committee

[*] Jane Cai and Daniel Ren, "Shanghai Vice-Mayor Set for China Investment Corp," *South China Morning Post*, May 11, 2013. http://www.scmp.com/business/banking-finance/article/1234975/shanghai-vice-mayor-set-cic.

in the fund's annual reports. Sources report that Chairman Lou served as the party secretary of the committee alongside his other duties. Executive directors Gao Xiqing and Hu Huaibang apparently served as vice secretaries in the committee.[133] CIC's new chairman will likely take the lead in the committee.

The presence of Chinese Communist Party officials on CIC's boards raises questions about the fund's compliance with the Santiago Principles. GAPP 16 calls for public disclosure of operational independence between management and the shareholder. CIC states that it is operationally independent from its shareholder, the State Council. However, as CIC's management is comprised of government officials who have direct or indirect relationships with the leadership of the State Council, it is difficult to adequately determine CIC's independence from political influence when making important decisions.

***Auditing and Disclosure of Domestic Investment Performance***

Financial auditing is a subtle but vital area in which CIC's transparency and accountability are at risk. The Santiago Principles (GAPP 12) recommend that SWFs conduct annual independent external audits.[134] A model for this is Norway's Government Pension Fund Global, which is currently audited by Deloitte, one of the "Big Four" international accounting firms.[135] However, CIC's "external auditor" is the China National Audit Office (CNAO), the Chinese government's supreme audit authority.[136] CNAO is a ministry directly under CIC's shareholder, the State Council.[137] CNAO's Deputy Auditor General Dong Dasheng also sits on CIC's board of supervisors.[138]

Due to its holdings in domestic financial institutions, managed by its subsidiary Central Huijin, CIC potentially falls short of meeting the recommendations of other GAPP principles. GAPP 17, for instance, calls for public disclosure of relevant financial information, including asset allocation, relevant benchmarks, and rates of return. Although CIC provides some financial information in greater detail than other SWFs, it does not include performance measures, such as annual returns, for its domestic portfolio. In August 2010, Central Huijin released a financial report covering the period between 2007 and 2009, part of disclosure rules for an issuance of RMB 160 billion worth of bonds on the interbank market.[139] Currently, however, the performance of CIC's domestic assets can only be extrapolated from the fund's overall investment returns, which include both domestic and outbound investment, and from the growth of the asset class known as "long-term equity," which connotes CIC's long-term domestic holdings under Central Huijin.

**Table 4-1. Transparency of China's SWFs (LMTI System)**

| SWF | LMTI | Rank |
|---|---|---|
| China Investment Corporation (CIC) | 7 | 23rd |
| National Social Security Fund (NSSF) | 5 | 31st |
| SAFE Investment Company (SAFEIC) | 4 | 34th |
| China-Africa Development (CAD) Fund | 4 | 38th |

Note: Rankings are deduced from a list of the world's 48 largest SWFs. Ratings given to SWFs are based on a point system of 1-10 determined by essential principles that depict transparency, with a score of 1 representing complete opaqueness and 10 representing complete transparency. The Sovereign Wealth Fund Institute recommends a minimum rating of 8 in order to claim adequate transparency.

Source: Sovereign Wealth Fund Institute, *4th Quarter 2012 LMTI ratings* (Las Vegas, NV), http://www.swfinstitute.org/statistics-research/linaburg-maduell-transparency-index.

## Regulatory Gaps in the International System

While assessing compliance with existing rules and norms, it is also important to recognize regulatory gaps in the international system. One gap is that the Santiago Principles are nonenforceable. Consequently, guidelines and policies are only as good as the commitment of the signatories. In the absence of private shareholders, the main incentive for CIC and other SWFs to abide by rules and norms is to improve perceptions in recipient countries. But this incentive may diminish as SWFs become more influential.

A second concern is that the Santiago Principles have not expanded to cover more SWFs. In China, no SWF other than CIC has signed on. Part of the problem is definitional – the framers of Santiago essentially concur with the Chinese government that CIC is the only fund that qualifies as an SWF.

Perhaps not surprisingly, China's other SWFs rank lower than CIC in standard governance scores. Of particular concern is SAFE, which has direct access to China's foreign exchange reserves. Although SAFE does publish an annual report, it does not provide detail on the activities of SAFEIC. That has left market analysts puzzled about which investments it has made and how. The *Financial Times* noted in 2008 that "several company representatives [in Hong Kong] confirmed that they were aware of the stakes held by Safe Investment Company but could not confirm the nature of the shareholding entity. The paper trail has been confused by various methods and names for purchasing stakes."[140] The only way the *Wall Street Journal* was able to trace

SAFEIC's investments in the United Kingdom was by looking at property deals and at disclosures by the companies that received the investments.[141] SAFE has also been reluctant to disclose details on its internal organization. It took until 2007 for it to confirm the existence of SAFEIC, even though this Hong Kong-based foreign investment arm was already created in 1997.[142] Similarly, SAFE took several months to confirm the existence of a new Co-Finance Office, established in 2011 to support China's outbound investors.[143]

Another loophole in international regulation relates to the entities that SWFs collaborate with. Failure to adequately regulate these actors has an indirect impact on the transparency of SWFs. Of particular concern is the "shadow banking" system, in which financial intermediaries do not accept traditional bank deposits, and thus are not subject to traditional banking regulations. Examples include hedge funds, unlisted derivatives, and other financial instruments not subject to regulatory oversight. According to one scholar, more information is known about the portfolio holdings of SWFs than large, private financial institutions, which have less reason to be concerned about public perceptions.[144] Although SWF managers have complained about receiving more scrutiny than hedge funds and other managers, there is also the potential for them to use external fund managers to make strategic investments in an opaque manner. CIC, which manages 57 percent of its portfolio through external managers,[145] has certainly resorted to this strategy, even if it began to manage more assets internally in 2010.

CIC also owns equity in and cooperates with China's state-owned enterprises and banks. A few years prior to the Santiago Principles, there were prospects for a binding international agreement on regulating state-owned enterprises to better reveal the nature of their operations and their ties to sovereign government interests.[146] At present, however, no such agreement has been implemented. Regulation of SWFs but not SOEs is especially problematic in China's case, where state actors are pervasive, and the divisions between them are blurred.

## SECTION 5: REGULATORY RESPONSES IN THE UNITED STATES

Over the past six years, China's SWFs have made major investments in the United States. CIC has become an active portfolio investor, pouring over $9 billion into 84 U.S.-traded public companies by the end of 2009, including brand names like Coca-Cola Company, Apple Inc., and Johnson & Johnson.[147] In addition, CIC has purchased larger interests in several U.S. companies, among them Blackstone, Morgan Stanley, and Blackrock in the financial sector, and AES in the energy sector. Although CIC has shifted more of its assets to other countries, the United States remains an important market.

The regulatory responses to CIC in the United States have been complex. As Robert H. Smith, business professor at the University of Maryland, told the USCC in 2008: "U.S. policy with regard to sovereign wealth is largely underdeveloped. It has to be discerned from a variety of laws and regulations."[148] Thus far, regulation of inbound investment from China's SWFs in the United States has been handled primarily by four agencies: the Federal Reserve (Fed) and the Securities and Exchange Commission (SEC) in the financial sector; the Committee on Foreign Investment in the United States (CFIUS) outside the financial sector; and Internal Revenue Service (IRS) tax regulations for foreign sovereign investors.

## CFIUS Exon-Florio Reviews

In recent years, CFIUS has developed into a major tool for U.S. regulators to screen foreign investments that have national security implications. The committee was established by Congress under the Exon-Florio Amendment of the Omnibus Trade and Competitiveness Act of 1988, which was added to Section 721 of the 1950 Defense Production Act. Prior to 1988, investments could only be blocked if the president declared a national emergency or if regulators invoked federal antitrust, environmental, or securities laws. Under the new law, CFIUS, an interagency committee chaired by the Treasury, could screen foreign investments on national security grounds, while the president was granted the authority to block or suspend a foreign takeover of U.S. firms based on "credible evidence" that it may "impair the national security." Crucially for SWFs, the Byrd Amendment to the Exon-Florio statute in 1992 required CFIUS to investigate investments in which the investor is controlled by a foreign government.[149]

In 2007, the Foreign Investment and National Security Act of 2007 (FINSA) significantly expanded the scope and intensity of the Exon-Florio review process. As a result of FINSA, CFIUS has become much more active. In 2008-11, average notifications per year rose by 24 percent over 1988-2005. The share of notices investigated has increased from 2 percent to 23 percent.[150]

Chinese companies too have been subject to the Exon-Florio review process. In 2005, the proposed takeover of U.S. oil company Unocal by China's oil major CNOOC was opposed by certain Members of Congress. That factored into CNOOC's decision to withdraw the proposal. In 2008-11, after FINSA was introduced, CFIUS reviewed 26 investments by Chinese companies. In three cases, CFIUS contributed to blocking these investments.[151]

Through 2012, CIC has made half a dozen large investments in U.S. firms but has only been reviewed once by CFIUS. In 2007, FINSA sponsor Senator Chris Dodd (D-CT) sought information to see if CIC's acquisition of Morgan Stanley required a CFIUS review.[152] Yet by buying stakes below 10 percent, CIC was not subject to the review. The fund was counseled in the matter by U.S. law firm Sullivan & Cromwell LLP.[153]

The exceptional case was AES Corp. In 2009, CIC purchased a 15 percent stake in the U.S. energy firm, prompting a drawn-out, four-month CFIUS review process. During this period, CIC's then Chairman Lou urged Washington to relax scrutiny of Chinese government entities investing in the United States and to speed up deals that might help create jobs for Americans.[154] Eventually, however, CIC utilized the AES case to demonstrate that it was a "responsible investor." It enlisted the support of Covington & Burlington, the same U.S. law firm that represented CNOOC during its CFIUS approval process in 2005.[155] CFIUS eventually approved the investment in 2010.

## Financial Sector Oversight

In the financial sector, CIC has come under more frequent review by U.S. regulators than it has in CFIUS. The SEC has been effective in getting CIC to disclose more information about its investments and operations. The regulator requires institutional investors to submit the form if they use the U.S. mail for business and exercise discretion over $100 million or more of "Section 13(f) securities". To date, CIC has made over 25 filings to the SEC. Most notably, in February 2010 a comprehensive list of CIC's holdings in U.S. publicly traded securities was made available to the public when it filed SEC Form 13F, a quarterly holdings report.[156]

CIC's 2010 filing did not include its entire stakes in the United States, such as its investment in Blackstone Group. But the filing was the first time

CIC has disclosed the quantity and value of its holdings of U.S. publicly traded securities, which at the time totaled US$9.63 billion.[157] It revealed some of CIC's largest holdings: Teck Resources ($3.5 billion), Morgan Stanley ($1.8 billion), Blackrock ($714 million), and smaller stakes in companies like AIG ($14.3 million), and Apple ($6.3 million).

The 2010 filing was the only instance in which CIC has disclosed holdings of U.S. securities in such detail. The fund has not filed another Form 13F since then. Nonetheless, CIC has continually made other routine filings with the SEC regarding transfer of beneficial ownership, which includes Schedule 13D, a filing required of any investor that acquires over 5 percent ownership of a voting class of a company's equity securities.[158]

The Federal Reserve, for its part, has reviewed CIC in two areas: (1) CIC's proposed acquisition of interest in U.S.-based financial institutions; and (2) proposed transactions in the United States by Chinese commercial banks, which are indirectly controlled by CIC through its wholly owned subsidiary, Central Huijin. So far, four cases involving CIC have been reviewed and approved by the Fed:

- *Industrial and Commercial Bank of China* (August 2008). ICBC, the commercial bank owned by CIC subsidiary Central Huijin, won approval for a U.S. banking license.
- *Morgan Stanley* (August 2010). CIC was granted permission to convert its shares in Morgan Stanley, purchased in 2007, into voting shares.
- *Industrial and Commercial Bank of China* (May 2012). ICBC, in which Central Huijin has a 35.5 percent stake, won approval to buy an 80 percent stake in the U.S. operations of Bank of East Asia.
- *Bank of China* and *Agricultural Bank of China* (May 2012). Bank of China, in which Central Huijin has a 67.7 percent stake, and ABC, in which Central Huijin has a 40.2 percent stake, were granted permission to open branches in New York and Chicago.

In reviewing these cases, the primary question has been how CIC should be treated under the U.S. Bank Holding Company Act (BHCA). Under the BHCA, a bank holding company is not permitted to purchase more than 5 percent of the shares of any nonbanking company, whether in the United States or anywhere else. Further, a bank holding company must be reviewed in tandem with any investments by its subsidiaries and must fulfill regular reporting, filing, and capitalization requirements. The aim is to prevent "moral hazard" and unfair competition, such as lending by a bank to a firm controlled by the same parent.* A bank holding company must also be reviewed in tandem with any regulatory review of the banks it controls. An entity is defined as a "bank holding company" if it influences the election of a majority of the bank's board members; owns 25 percent or more of its voting shares; or has the ability to exercise a "controlling influence" through management.[159]

When the BHCA was first enacted in 1956, it applied exclusively to domestic banks. In 1978, Congress passed the International Banking Act (IBA) to ensure that the BHCA applied equally to any foreign bank that operates a branch, agency, or commercial lending company in the United States, and any company that controls the foreign bank.[160] In 1988, the Fed's treatment of a state-owned Italian bank also set an important precedent by maintaining that legal entities established or controlled by foreign governments are "companies" for BHCA purposes. In 1991, the IBA was further amended to give the Fed stronger supervision and enforcement rights vis-à-vis foreign banks; in particular, the establishment of a U.S. branch by a foreign bank required Fed approval.[161]

If strictly enforced, the above regulations would put CIC in a difficult position. CIC's designation as a bank holding company would bar it from investing in nonbank assets, a practically inconceivable restriction given the fund's existing holdings and planned investments in other sectors. On the other hand, if CIC were to engage in nonbanking activities, the Chinese banks it controls could be barred from doing business in the United States. The BHCA reporting requirements would also hamper CIC's decision-making and potentially force it and Central Huijin to disclose information about Chinese banks that is closely guarded by the Chinese government.[162]

However, in approving the U.S. activities of ICBC, BOC, and ABC, the Fed ultimately took a lenient approach. It not only approved the proposed transactions but also allowed CIC to go on for the most part with business as usual. The Fed made extensive use of Section 4(c)(9) of the BHCA, under which it has wide discretion to offer exemptions. In its approval of ICBC's banking license in autumn 2008, the Fed recognized both CIC and Central Huijin as bank holding companies. Yet in so doing, it did not place any

* Moral hazard occurs when a party to a transaction takes unusual risks in order to earn a profit, knowing that the costs of such a risk will be borne by another party.

restrictions on CIC's nonbank investments. In addition, the Fed largely exempted CIC and Central Huijin from the regular reporting, filing, and capitalization requirements of the BHCA.[163]

According to Robert Pozen, a professor at the Harvard Business School, Central Huijin extensively supported ICBC during and after the global financial crisis, indicating "significant involvement in ICBC's management of its finances."[164] Guo Li, a legal scholar at China's Tsinghua University, has noted: "Thanks to the Fed's conditional exemptions, the CIC invested with more autonomy in areas such as commodities, real estate, and infrastructure [...] in addition to the financial sector."[165]

An analysis published by the Tufts Sovereign Wealth Fund Initiative further illustrated the exceptional nature of the exemption vis-à-vis other SWFs:

> The upshot of the May 9, 2012 [ICBC] approval is that CIC and Huijin will now be able to register as bank holding companies. Until this time, other well publicized investments by sovereign wealth funds in foreign banks with US branches, and in US banks, have been specifically structured to avoid 'control' of a US bank, thereby avoiding having to register as a bank holding company under the BHC Act. For example, during the height of the financial crisis in 2008, Temasek Holdings (Private) Limited took great pains to structure its investment in Citigroup as non-controlling, thereby avoiding the need to seek FRB [Federal Reserve Bank] approval to become a bank holding company. In contrast, CIC and Huijin actually sought approval from the FRB to become bank holding companies as well as exemptions from limitations on non-banking activities available to foreign entities.[166]

The Fed did place some conditions on its exemptions:

- CIC and Central Huijin must continue to do a majority of their business outside the United States.
- CIC and Central Huijin must inform the Fed of any acquisition of 25 percent or more of any company that has activities in the United States, as well as any acquisition of 5 percent or more of a company that engages in financial holding activities in the United States.
- ICBC's U.S. branch can do business with other companies controlled by CIC, but transactions with a single controlled company are limited

to 10 percent of the branch's lending base, and transactions with all controlled companies cannot exceed 20 percent of the lending base.

- The foreign bank subsidiaries of China's banks cannot engage in any cross-marketing of goods and services with companies controlled by CIC.
- The Fed reserves the right to come up with new requirements for supervising the banks over time; for instance, future investments by CIC can be assessed for conflict of interest.[167]

In addition to the exemption under the BHCA, the Fed was very generous in its interpretation of financial supervision in China. The Fed must demonstrate that any of the banks it approves conform to comprehensive and consolidated supervision criteria. That essentially means that home country regulators are able to monitor and control a bank's overseas activities; are sufficiently informed about its financial condition through both audits and consolidated reports of its worldwide activities; and are aware of all its transactions with its affiliates at home and abroad. The Fed was evidently concerned about China's ability to meet the comprehensive and consolidated supervision criteria, given its heavy state ownership; the poor quality of Chinese banks' loan portfolios; lax risk management; and widespread fraud. However, in granting the approvals, the Fed deemed China to be "actively working to establish" such supervision.[168]

The approval of CIC's share conversion in Morgan Stanley was another important test case for financial regulation of a Chinese SWF. In a positive sense, the Fed asserted its authority to approve such transactions. CIC's initial investment in 2007 did not require BHCA approval, and CIC took special care to keep its share in the firm below 10 percent so as not to be considered an active investor. But in 2010, CIC still had to seek Fed approval when it converted its share in Morgan Stanley into voting shares. The justification, according to the Fed, was that both CIC and Morgan Stanley had been converted into bank holding companies under U.S. law – the Fed required approval for any CIC investment in a U.S. bank holding company above 5 percent.[169]

Although the Fed expanded its approval powers in this case, its decision was again lenient. While it recognized CIC as a "government-owned investment company organized to invest the foreign exchange reserves of the government", it did not find this to have any impact on CIC's financial and managerial resources. The Fed argued that the diverse representation of government agencies on CIC's board, and the "periodic external audits" conducted by China's National Audit Office, were sufficient to show that "appropriate authorities in China would appear to have full access to and oversight of CIC and its activities."[170] The Fed approval document contained no special analysis related to sovereign wealth funds or regulatory concerns regarding a foreign government as a controlling stockholder.[171]

## Internal Revenue Service Tax Exemptions

While CIC has demanded to be treated like a private investor by CFIUS and the Fed, its status as a sovereign investor may also be reducing its tax burden under U.S. law. In section 892(a)(1) of the Internal Revenue Code, the income of foreign governments received from stocks, bonds, or other domestic securities is exempt from taxation. The rule was presumably introduced for central banks acting as passive investors in the United States. However, with the advent of aggressive investment by SWFs, the rule has become more controversial.[172]

At present, CIC and other SWFs are still treated as "foreign governments" under U.S. tax law. As such, their investments in stocks, bonds, or other domestic securities are still tax exempt under certain conditions. The exemption has even been expanded to account for the growing commercial activity of SWFs. Under the original law, any "commercial activity income" by an entity controlled by the SWF makes that entity subject to full taxation.[173] In 2008, Senator Max Baucus (D.-MT), then chairman of the Senate Committee on Finance, and Senator Chuck Grassley (R.-IA), then the ranking member, requested that the nonpartisan Joint Committee on Taxation review the tax policy on sovereign investors. They reasoned that "[due to] the rapid increase in the size and number of SWFs, their U.S. investments, and their expected continued growth, it is appropriate to examine the tax regime applicable to their U.S. investments and its policy underpinnings."[174]

In November 2011, the IRS proposed regulations to make it easier for foreign governments to avoid taxation. The new rules mandate that SWFs will no longer be regarded as "commercial entities" simply because they hold interest as a limited partner in a limited partnership. Rather, SWFs can engage in commercial activities and remain tax exempt as long as their commercial activities do not exceed 5 percent of their gross income or their assets in a commercial entity are less than 5 percent of their total assets. Further, investments in financial instruments will not be treated as commercial activities whether or not the instruments are held in the execution of financial or monetary policy. Nor will profits from the sale of a U.S. real property be constituted as commercial activity. [175]

## Conclusion

In less than a decade, China's SWFs have become major actors in the global economy. China is only one of many countries that have developed SWFs; yet it is also an outlier. China has the world's largest foreign exchange reserves, several SWFs, and by some counts, one-quarter of global SWF assets. It could be recycling the dollars it has earned from the international economy into the domestic economy, a process that would potentially redistribute wealth and stimulate consumption. But China's monetary and industrial policy remains focused on encouraging exports and keeping factors of production – notably capital – in state hands. That has led to a buildup of foreign exchange reserves and provided incentives for using SWFs.

Even if China's SWFs continue to expand, their strategic orientation remains vague. CIC has only managed a very small portion of China's foreign exchange reserves and has faced competition from other state-sponsored entities. It has yet to establish a stable funding mechanism, and has had trouble finding a successor for former Chairman Lou Jiwei. The fund has made efforts to become more professional, but the presence of officials in the senior management suggests that at least some of the fund's decisions are politicized. Engagement in strategic sectors, coordination with SOEs, and economic diplomacy further suggest that CIC's motives are not strictly commercial.

Concerns about China's SWFs in the U.S. economy could be addressed in several ways:

- *Promote economic reform in China.* The U.S. government, through the Strategic and Economic Dialogue and other mechanisms, could urge China to revalue its currency and reduce its current account surplus. As C. Fred Bergsten of the Peterson Institute has noted in new research, currency manipulation has been one of the major impediments to fixing the global economy.[176] Economic reform will reduce China's buildup of foreign currency reserves and its incentive to expand SWF investments. The net benefits to the United States of China's economic rebalancing will outweigh the value to the United States of China's SWF investment.

- *Urge CIC to clarify its holdings and investment strategy.* CIC's holdings in state-owned commercial banks in China, coupled with its lack of transparency in specifying its shareholder and management relations with the government, violate the spirit of the Santiago Principles and may pose a risk to the global financial sector. Even in China, academics and journalists have expressed concern about the lack of binding rules and laws for the fund.[177] The Fed's conditional exemptions under the Bank Holding Company Act may have set a negative precedent for dealing with this issue.
- *Increase CFIUS oversight.* In 2012, the USCC recommended that Congress consider (1) requiring a mandatory review of all controlling transactions by Chinese state-owned and state-controlled companies investing in the United States; (2) adding a net economic benefit test to the existing national security test that CFIUS administers; and (3) prohibiting investment in a U.S. industry by a foreign company whose government prohibits foreign investment in that same industry."[178] These recommendations could be relevant for reviewing the investments of CIC and its banking affiliates in the United States.
- *Further develop the Santiago framework.* The GAPP principles encourage transparency among SWFs but are nonbinding and do not cover all SWFs, let alone other state-sponsored entities. The framework could be made more intensive and extensive. It could also foster more dialogue with SWF countries through the SWFI and IFSWF.
- *Regulate hedge funds and other fund managers.* As China's SWFs outsource to and buy equity in fund management companies, the U.S. government should remain informed about the nature of these partnerships in order to preempt a buildup of sovereign wealth in the "shadow banking" system.

# APPENDIX

**Table A-1. Varying Definitions of a Sovereign Wealth Fund**

| | |
|---|---|
| • **International Monetary Fund** | SWFs are government-owned investment funds set up for a variety of macroeconomic purposes. |
| • **International Working Group on Sovereign Wealth Funds (Santiago Principles)** | SWFs are defined as special purpose investment funds or arrangements, owned by the general government. Created by the general government for macroeconomic purposes, SWFs hold, manage, or administer assets to achieve financial objectives and employ a set of investment strategies that include investing in foreign financial assets. The SWFs are commonly established out of balance of payments surpluses, official foreign currency operations, the proceeds of privatizations, fiscal surpluses, and/or receipts resulting from commodity exports. |
| • **Organization for Economic Cooperation and Development** | SWFs are pools of assets owned and managed directly or indirectly by governments to achieve national objectives. |
| • **Sovereign Wealth Fund Institute** | A SWF is a state-owned investment fund or entity that is commonly established from balance of payments surpluses, official foreign currency operations, the proceeds of privatization, governmental transfer payments, fiscal surpluses, and/or receipts resulting from resource exports. The definition of sovereign wealth fund excludes, among other things, foreign currency reserve assets held by monetary authorities for the traditional balance of payments or monetary policy purposes, state-owned enterprises in the traditional sense, government-employee pension funds (funded by employee/employer contributions), or assets managed for the benefit of individuals. |
| • **U.S. Department of the Treasury** | SWFs are investment vehicles funded by foreign exchange assets and managed separately from official reserves. |
| • **Ashby H.B. Monk, Boston College** | SWFs are government-owned and -controlled (directly or indirectly) investment funds that have no outside liabilities or beneficiaries (beyond the government or the citizenry in abstract) and that invest their assets, either in the short or long term, according to the interests and objectives of the sponsoring government. |

**Table A-2. Comparison of China's Sovereign Wealth Funds**

| | **SAFE Investment Company (Hua'An)** | **National Social Security Fund (NSSF)** | **China Investment Corporation (CIC)** | **China-Africa Development Fund (CADF)** |
|---|---|---|---|---|
| **Year Established** | 1997 | 2000 | 2007 | 2007 |
| **Assets ($ billions)** | $568 | $140 | $487 | $5 (initial capital) |
| **Official objectives** | Diversify foreign exchange reserves in order to reduce risks of fluctuations in value of the U.S. dollar. Do so primarily through acquisition of low-risk assets, like U.S. treasuries. | Strategic reserve fund accumulated by the central government to support future social security expenditures and other social security needs. Aim is to retain and increase the real value of pension funds | Diversify foreign exchange reserves by maximizing returns on risk-adjusted investments. | Promote African economic development through subsidized credit. |
| **Locations** | Hong Kong | Beijing | Beijing; Toronto; Hong Kong | Beijing |
| **Legal basis** | Registed as a Hong Kong limited company | Established under Article 71 of the *Social Insurance Law of the People's Republic of China* | Incorporated under *China Corporate Law* | Created after approval by the State Council of CDB-sponsored *China- African Development Fund Establishment Plan* |
| **Owner** | People's Bank of China (PBOC) | National Council for Social Security Fund | State Council | China Development Bank |

|  | **SAFE Investment Company (Hua'An)** | **National Social Security Fund (NSSF)** | **China Investment Corporation (CIC)** | **China-Africa Development Fund (CADF)** |
| --- | --- | --- | --- | --- |
| **Governance** | • Run as a branch of the Reserve Management Department of the State Administration of Foreign Exchange (SAFE), under the PBOC.<br>• One of SAFE's four foreign investment arms - Hua'An is based in Hong Kong, the other arms are in London, New York, and Singapore. | • Run as a department of the NCSSF, which is a ministry-level agency | • Independent unit, with some day-to-day affairs overseen, by the Ministry of Finance (MOF)<br>• However, CIC is equivalent in rank to a ministry, reports directly to the State Council, and receives its personnel appointments from the State Council | • Run as a branch of the China Development Bank |
| **Board composition** | Managed by a board of directors comprised of top officials from SAFE | • Managed by a board of directors appointed by the State Council<br>• Chairman is usually a retired official from the MOF | Includes government officials from numerous financial sector agencies, including MOF, China Banking Regulatory Commisison, and the central bank | Includes leaders of the CDB, and officials from various ministries (MOF, MOFCOM, and the NDRC) |

**Table A-3. Global Fund Management Industry**

| *US$ trillions* | | 2003 | 2005 | 2007 | 2009 | 2011 | Compound annual growth rate (%) |
|---|---|---|---|---|---|---|---|
| Conventional | (Pension, mutual, and insurance funds) | 46.9 | 58.9 | 76.4 | 71.3 | 79.8 | 7% |
| Non-conventional | **Sovereign Wealth Funds** | **1.5** | **2.3** | **3.7** | **3.8** | **4.8** | **16%** |
| | Private equity | 1.0 | 1.2 | 2.2 | 2.5 | 2.2 | 11% |
| | Hedge funds | 0.9 | 1.4 | 2.2 | 1.7 | 1.9 | 11% |
| | Exchange-Traded Funds | 0.2 | 0.4 | 0.7 | 1.0 | 1.4 | 30% |
| | Private wealth | 28.5 | 33.3 | 40.7 | 39.0 | 42.0 | 5% |
| | TOTAL | 78.8 | 97.4 | 125.8 | 119.3 | 132.1 | 7% |

| *Composition (%)* | | 2003 | 2005 | 2007 | 2009 | 2011 | Change 2003-2011 |
|---|---|---|---|---|---|---|---|
| Conventional | (Pension, mutual, and insurance funds) | 59.5% | 60.5% | 60.7% | 59.8% | 60.4% | 0.9% |
| Non-conventional | **Sovereign Wealth Funds** | **1.9%** | **2.4%** | **3.0%** | **3.2%** | **3.6%** | **1.8%** |
| | Private equity | 1.2% | 1.3% | 1.7% | 2.1% | 1.7% | 0.4% |
| | Hedge funds | 1.1% | 1.4% | 1.7% | 1.4% | 1.4% | 0.4% |
| | Exchange-Traded Funds | 0.2% | 0.4% | 0.6% | 0.8% | 1.1% | 0.8% |
| | Private wealth | 36.1% | 34.2% | 32.3% | 32.7% | 31.8% | -4.4% |
| | TOTAL | 59.5% | 60.5% | 60.7% | 59.8% | 60.4% | 0.9% |

Source: The City-UK estimates. http://stagingtcuk.positive-technology.com/research/ our-work/reports-list/fund- management-2010/.

**Table A-4. Sovereign Wealth Fund Rankings (SWFI Estimates, 2011)**

| Rank | Country | SWF Name | Assets (US$ billion) | Inception | Origin |
|---|---|---|---|---|---|
| 1 | Norway | Government Pension Fund - Global | 664.3 | 1990 | Oil |
| 2 | UAE-Abu Dhabi | Abu Dhabi Investment Authority | 627.0 | 1976 | Oil |
| **3** | **China** | **SAFE Investment Company** | **567.9** | **1997** | **Non-Commodity** |
| 4 | Saudi Arabia | SAMA Foreign Holdings | 532.8 | n/a | Oil |
| **5** | **China** | **China Investment Corporation** | **482.0** | **2007** | **Non-Commodity** |
| 6 | China-Hong Kong | Hong Kong Monetary Authority Investment Portfolio | 298.7 | 1993 | Non-Commodity |
| 7 | Kuwait | Kuwait Investment Authority | 296.0 | 1953 | Oil |
| 8 | Singapore | Government of Singapore Investment Corporation | 247.5 | 1981 | Non-Commodity |
| 9 | Singapore | Temasek Holdings | 157.5 | 1974 | Non-Commodity |
| 10 | Russia | National Welfare Fund | 149.7 | 2008 | Oil |
| | … | | | | |
| **11** | **China** | **National Social Security Fund** | **134.5** | **2000** | **Non-Commodity** |
| **43** | **China** | **China-Africa Development Fund** | **5.0** | **2007** | **Non-Commodity** |
| | | Total Oil & Gas Related | 2,991.4 | | |
| | | Total Other | 2,214.5 | | |
| | | TOTAL | 5,205.9 | | |

Source: Sovereign Wealth Fund Institute. http://www.swfinstitute.org/fund-rankings/.

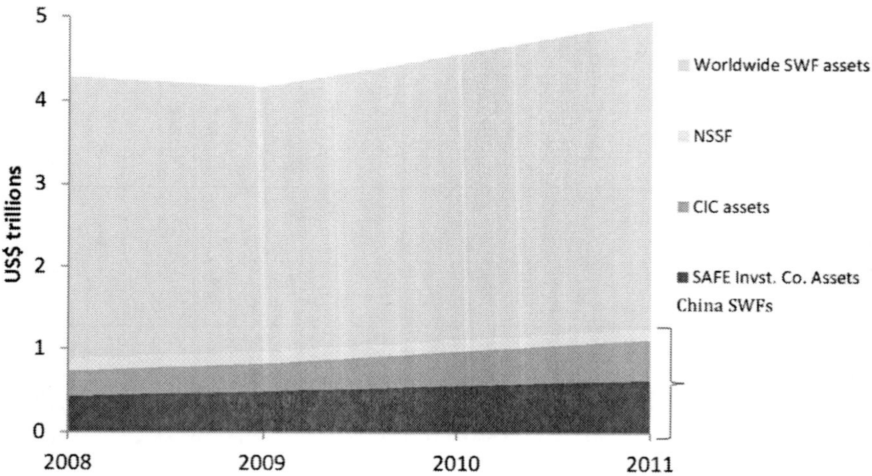


Note: National Social Security Fund (NSSF) assets based on original registered capital. Sources: Sovereign Wealth Fund Institute. http://www.swfinstitute.org/fund-rankings/; *China Investment Corporation, 2008-2011 Annual Reports (Beijing, China).*

Figure A-1. Worldwide SWF Assets, 2008-2011.

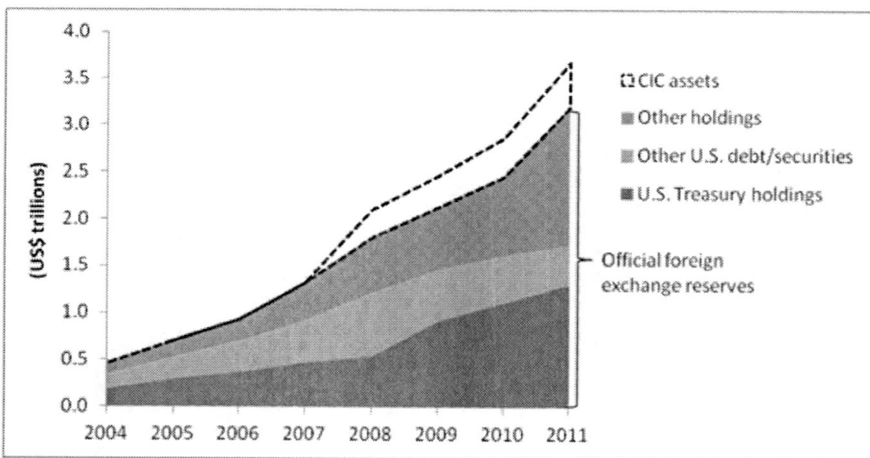


Sources: U. S. Department of the Treasury, PBOC, CIC annual reports.

Figure A-2. CIC Assets in Relation to Official Reserves.

**Table A-5. Holdings of Central Huijin**

| | Core Business | Company Name | Type of Entity | Percentage (%) | | Core Business | Company Name | Type of Entity | Percentage (%) |
|---|---|---|---|---|---|---|---|---|---|
| 1 | Assets Management | Jiantou Zhongxin Assets Management Co, Ltd. | Limited liability | 70.0 | 10 | Investments | China Jianyin Investment Limited | Wholly State-owned | 100.0 |
| 2 | Banking | Bank of China Limited | Joint Stock | 67.6 | 11 | Investments | China Everbright Industry Group Limited | Wholly State-owned | 100.0 |
| 3 | Banking | China Construction Bank Corporation | Joint Stock | 57.1 | 12 | Investments | China Galaxy Financial Holdings Co., Ltd. | Joint Stock | 78.6 |
| 4 | Banking | China Everbright Bank Co., Ltd. | Joint Stock | 48.7 | 13 | Securities | China Investment Securities Co., Ltd | Wholly State-owned | 100.0 |
| 5 | Banking | China Development Bank Corporation | Joint Stock | 47.6 | 14 | Securities | China International Capital Co., Ltd. | Limited liability | 43.4 |
| 6 | Banking | Agricultural Bank of China Limited | Joint Stock | 40.1 | 15 | Securities | China Securities Co., Ltd. | Joint Stock Company | 40.0 |
| 7 | Banking | Industrial and Commercial Bank of China Limited | Joint Stock | 35.4 | 16 | Securities | Shenyin & Wanguo Securities Co., Ltd | Joint Stock | 37.2 |
| 8 | Insurance | China Reinsurance (Group) Corporation | Joint Stock | 84.9 | 17 | Securities | Guotai junan Securities Co., Ltd. | Joint Stock | 21.3 |
| 9 | Insurance | New China Life Insurance Co., Ltd. | Joint Stock | 31.3 | 18 | Securities | UBS Securities Co., Ltd. | Limited liability | 14.0 |

Source: "investments," Central Huijin Ltd. website, http://www.huijin-inv.cn/hjen/investments/popup.htm.

**Table A-6. Major CIC Transactions with Outside Fund Managers**

| Equity Stakes in Fund Managers | | | | | | |
|---|---|---|---|---|---|---|
| **Year** | **Month** | **Firm Type** | **Firm** | **Country** | **Amount (US$ millions)** | **Size of share (%)** |
| 2007 | May | Private equity | Blackstone | USA | $3,030 | 9.4% |
| 2007 | Dec | Investment bank | Morgan Stanley | USA | $5,000 | 9.9% |
| 2008 | Oct | Private equity | Blackstone | USA | $200 | 3.0% |
| 2009 | Jun | Investment bank | Morgan Stanley | USA | $1,210 | 1.0% |
| 2009 | Jun | Private equity | Blackrock | USA | $1,000 | 3.0% |
| 2009 | Jul | Investment bank | CITIC Capital | China (HK) | $250 | 40.0% |
| 2009 | Sep | Investment bank | Poly (Hong Kong) Investments Ltd. | China (HK) | $53 | 2.8% |
| 2010 | Feb | Private equity | Apax Finance | UK | $960 | 2.3% |
| 2010 | May | Commodity fund | Penn West Energy | Canada | $435 | 5.0% |
| 2010 | Dec | Investment bank | BTG Pactual | Brazil | $300 | 3.1% |
| 2011 | Feb | Private equity | VTB Group | Russia | $100 | 5.0% |
| 2011 | Dec | Commodity fund | Shanduka Group | South Africa | $250 | 25.1% |
| 2011 | Dec | Middle-market Germany equities | Deutsche Bank (New Germany Fund Inc.) | USA | n.a. | 5.0% |
| 2012 | Feb | Commodity fund | EIG Global Energy Partners | USA | n.a. | n.a. |

**Financing of Fund Vehicles**

| Year | Month | Fund Type | Firm | Country | Amount (US$ millions) | |
|---|---|---|---|---|---|---|
| 2008 | Apr | Private equity | JC Flowers | USA | $3,200 | |
| 2008 | Sep | Mutual fund | Reserve Primary Fund | USA | $5,400 | |
| 2009 | Mar | Investment banking | Morgan Stanley | USA | $800 | |
| 2009 | Jun | Private equity | Blackstone | USA | $500 | |
| 2009 | Aug | Hedge fund (fixed-income) | Capula Investment Management LLP | | $200 | |
| 2009 | Sep | Hedge fund (fixed-income/ distressed) | Oaktree Capital Management | USA | $600 | |
| 2009 | Sep | Real estate fund (distressed) | Goldman Sachs | USA | $600 | |
| 2010 | Feb | Commodity fund | State Street Advisors (SPDR Gold Trust) | USA | $156 | |
| 2010 | Feb | Commodity fund | U.S. Oil Fund | USA | $79 | |
| 2010 | Feb | Private equity | Apax Partners | UK | $1,200 | |
| 2010 | Feb | Private equity | Lexington Partners | USA | $500 | |
| 2010 | Feb | Private equity | Pantheon Venture | USA | $500 | |
| 2010 | Feb | Private equity | Goldman Sachs | USA | $500 | |
| 2010 | Mar | Commodity fund | Brookfield | Canada | $200 | |
| 2010 | May | Commodity fund | Penn West Energy | Canada | $817 | |
| 2011 | Feb | Investment banking | Morgan Stanley | Japan | $190 | |
| 2011 | Oct | Private equity | Russian Direct Investment Fund | Russia | $1,000 | |
| 2012 | Apr | Private equity | Blackrock (to be launched 2013) | USA | $200 | |

**Table A-7. Chronology of Major CIC Investments (Excluding Investment Funds)**

| Year | Month | Amount (S millions) | Share Size | Partner/Target | Sector | Subsector | Country |
|---|---|---|---|---|---|---|---|
| **2007** | **May** | **$3,030** | **9.4%** | **Blackstone** | **Finance** | **Investment** | **USA** |
| 2007 | Nov | $100 | 4.0% | China Railway Group | Transport | | China (HK) |
| **2007** | **Dec** | **$5,600** | **9.9%** | **Morgan Stanley** | **Finance** | **Investment** | **USA** |
| **2008** | **Mar** | **$100** | **0.5%** | **Visa** | **Finance** | | **USA** |
| **2008** | **Oct** | **$200** | **3.0%** | **Blackstone** | **Finance** | **Investment** | **USA** |
| **2009** | **Jun** | **$1,210** | **1.0%** | **Morgan Stanley** | **Finance** | **Banking** | **USA** |
| **2009** | **Jun** | **$714** | **-** | **Blackrock** | **Finance** | **Investment** | **USA** |
| 2009 | Jul | $1,500 | 17.2% | Teck Resources | Metals | Copper | Canada |
| 2009 | Jul | $250 | 40.0% | CITIC Capital | Finance | Banking | China (HK) |
| 2009 | Jul | $370 | 1.0% | Diageo | Agriculture | | Britain |
| 2009 | Aug | $450 | 19.0% | Songbird Estates | Real estate | Property | Britain |
| 2009 | Aug | $1,090 | 6.9% | Goodman Group | Real estate | Property | Australia |
| 2009 | Sep | $940 | 10.6% | JSC KazMunaiGas E&P | Energy | Oil & gas | Kazakhstan |
| 2009 | Sep | $1,900 | - | PT Bumi Resources | Energy | | Indonesia |
| 2009 | Sep | $858 | 14.9% | Noble Group Limited | Agriculture | | Singapore |
| 2009 | Oct | $500.00 | - | Iron Mining International | Metals | | Hong Kong |
| 2009 | Oct | $250 | 13.0% | South Gobi Energy Resource Ltd. | Energy | Coal | Canada |
| 2009 | Oct | $270 | 45.0% | Nobel Oil Group LTD | Energy | Oil | Russian Federation |
| **2009** | **Nov** | **$1,580** | **15.0%** | **AES** | **Energy** | | **USA** |

| Year | Month | Amount (S millions) | Share Size | Partner/Target | Sector | Subsector | Country |
|---|---|---|---|---|---|---|---|
| 2009 | Nov | $717 | 20.1% | GCL-Poly Energy Holdings Ltd. | Energy | | Hong Kong |
| 2009 | Nov | $400 | - | Longyuan Power Group | Energy | | Hong Kong |
| 2009 | Dec | $500 | - | CVRD (Vale) | Metals | Steel | Brazil |
| 2010 | Mar | $816 | 15.8% | Changsha Zoomlion | Manufacturing | | China (HK) |
| 2010 | Jun | $329 | - | Peace River Oil Partnership JV | Energy | Oil & gas | Canada |
| **2010** | **Jun** | **$200** | | **Chesapeake Energy Corp.** | **Energy** | **Oil & gas** | **USA** |
| **2010** | **Nov** | **$1,030** | **7.4%** | **General Growth Properties** | **Real estate** | **Property** | **USA** |
| 2010 | Dec | $300 | 3.1% | BTG Pactual | Finance | Investment | Brazil |
| 2011 | Feb | $100 | 5.0% | VTB Group | Finance | Banking | Russian Federation |
| 2011 | Apr | $250 | 11.6% | Semiconductor Manufacturing International Corp. | Manufacturing | Electronics | China (NYSE listed) |
| 2011 | Jul | $100 | 10.5% | Diamond S Shipping | Transport | Shipping | Global |
| 2011 | Aug | $3,150 | 30.0% | GDF Suez | Energy | | France |
| 2011 | Sep | $93 | 19.0% | AES-VCM Mong Duong Power Co. Ltd. | Energy | Coal | Vietnam |
| 2011 | Oct | $300 | 13.8% | Horizon Roads (ConnectEast) | Transport | | Australia |
| 2011 | Nov | $850 | 10.0% | Atlantic LNG Company | Energy | | Trinidad-Tobago |
| 2011 | Dec | $800 | 50.0% | Global Logsistic Properties-CIC JV | Real estate | Property | Japan |

**Table A-7. (Continued)**

| Year | Month | Amount (S millions) | Share Size | Partner/Target | Sector | Subsector | Country |
|---|---|---|---|---|---|---|---|
| 2011 | Dec | $243 | 25.1% | Shanduka Group | Finance | Investment | South Africa |
| 2012 | Jan | $920 | 8.7% | Thames Water | Agriculture | | Britain |
| 2012 | Feb | $150 | 7.4% | Sunshine Oilsands | Energy | | Canada |
| 2012 | May | $420 | 5.0% | Polyus Gold | Metals | | Russian Federation |
| 2012 | Jun | $490 | 7.0% | Eutelsat | Technology | Telecom | France |
| **2012** | **Aug** | **$500** | - | **Cheniere Energy** | **Energy** | **Oil & gas** | **USA** |
| 2012 | Oct | $730 | 10.0% | Heathrow Ltd. (Heathrow Airport) | Transport | Aviation | Britain |
| 2012 | Nov | $400 | - | Deutsche Bank | Real estate | Property | Britain |
| 2012 | Nov | $110 | 13.0% | Brookfield Asset Management | Agriculture | Timber | Canada |
| 2012 | Nov | $460 | 34.5% | Global Logistic Properties | Real estate | Property | Brazil |

Sources: The Heritage Foundation, *China Global Investment Tracker* dataset (Washington, DC: updated January 2013). http://www.heritage.org/research/projects/china-global-investment-tracker-interactive-map; *Eiichi Sekine, "China Investment Corporation: Investment Performance in 2010 and Outlook," Nomura Journal of Capital Markets* 3:3 (Winter 2012) 6; Various news sources.

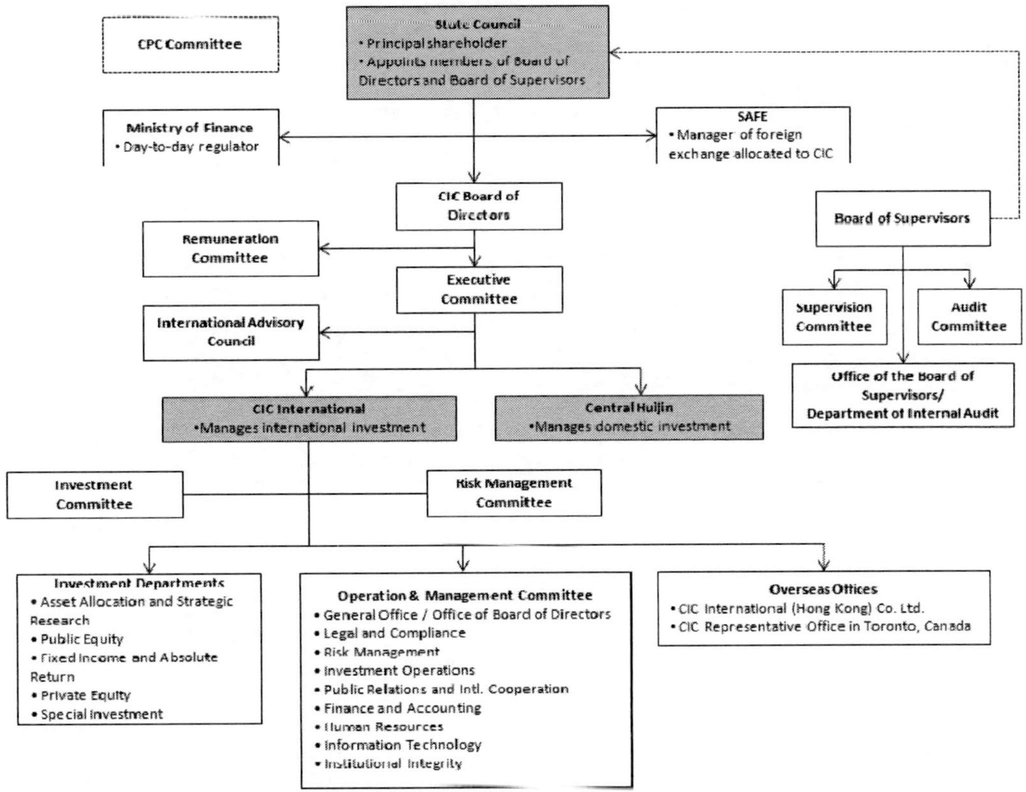


Sources: CIC annual reports, various news sources.

Figure A-3. CIC Organizational Structure.

## Table A-8. CIC Board Members and Their Current and Former Roles

| CIC Position | Name | Current or former role outside of CIC |
|---|---|---|
| **Board of Directors** | | |
| Chairman & CEO | TBD | |
| Vice Chairman & President | Gao Xiqing (高西庆) | Former Vice Chairman, National Council for the Social Security Fund; Vice Chairman of CSRC |
| Executive Director, Executive VP & CIO | Li Keping (李克平) | Former Vice Chairman, National Council for the Social Security Fund |
| Independent Directors | Liu Zhongli (刘仲藜) | Former Minister of Finance; Former Chairman, CPPCC Subcommittee of Economy |
| | Wang Chunzheng (王春正) | Former Head, Leading Group for Financial and Economic Affairs; Vice Minister, NDRC |
| Non-Executive Directors | Zhang Xiaoqiang (张晓强) | Current Vice Chairman, NDRC |
| | Li Yong (李勇) | Current Vice Minister of Finance |
| | Chen Jian (陈健) | Current Vice Minister of Commerce |
| | Hu Xiaolian (胡晓炼) | Current Deputy Governor, PBOC |
| | Fang Shangpu (方上浦) | Current Deputy Administer, SAFE |
| Employee Director | Li Xin (李炘) | Former Deputy Director, Commission for Science, Technology and Industry for National Defense; division chief at the Ministry of Finance |
| **Board of Supervisors** | | |
| Chairman of the Board of Supervisors | Li Xiaopeng (李晓鹏) | Former Vice President of ICBC |
| Supervisors | Dong Dasheng (董大胜) | Current Deputy Auditor General, National Audit Office |
| | Zhou Mubing (周慕冰) | Current Vice Chairman, China Banking Regulatory Commission |
| | Zhuang Xinyi (庄心一) | Current Vice Chairman, China Securities Regulatory Commission |
| Employee Supervisor | Cui Guangqing (崔光庆) | Former Director General, Information and Postal Audit Office, of the National Audit Office |
| **Executive Committee** | | |
| Chairman & CEO | TBD | |
| Vice Chairman & President | Gao Xiqing (高西庆) | Former Vice Chairman, National Council for the Social Security Fund; Vice Chairman of CSRC |
| Executive Director, Executive VP & CIO | Li Keping (李克平) | Former Vice Chairman, National Council for the Social Security Fund |
| Chairman of the Board of Supervisors | Li Xiaopeng (李晓鹏) | Former Vice President of ICBC |

| CIC Position | Name | Current or former role outside of CIC |
|---|---|---|
| Executive Vice President | Peng Chun (彭纯) | Former Executive Director and Executive Vice President of the Bank of Communications |
| Executive Vice President | Fan Yifei (范一飞) | Former Executive Vice President of the China Construction Bank (CCB) |
| Executive Vice President | Xie Ping (谢平) | Former Chairman of Shenyin & Wanguo Securities Co. Ltd.; Formerly held numerous positions at PBOC |
| Executive Vice President | Wang Jianxi "Jesse Wang" (汪建熙) | Former Deputy Chairman of China International Capital Corporation; Former Assistant Chairman of CSRC |
| Executive Vice President & Secretary of Discipline Inspecting Commission | Liang Xiang (梁骧) | Former Secretary of Discipline Inspecting Commission in the Export-Import Bank of China |
| Chief Strategy Officer | Zhou Yuan (周元) | Former Executive Vice Chairman of Hong Kong Mercantile Exchange |
| Chief Risk Officer | Guo Xiangjun (郭向军) | Former Deputy Director General of the Department of Fiscal and Financial Affairs of the NDRC; Former Deputy Director General of the Macroeconomic Control Department of the State Council Office for Restructuring the Economic System |
| Chief Information Technology Officer | Hua Hua (华桦) | Former Vice President of Great Wall Software International Ltd. |
| Member of the Executive Committee | Zhao Haiying (赵海英) | Former Deputy Director of the Department of Securities Issuance Supervision at CSRC |

Sources: China Investment Corporation, *Annual Report 2011* (Beijing, China: 2012); various news sources.

## Table A-9. CIC's Adherence to Santiago Principles on Public Disclosure

| GAPP | Principle/Subprinciple | Adherence |
|---|---|---|
| GAPP 1 | GAPP 1.2 Subprinciple: The key features of the SWF's legal basis and structure, as well as the legal relationship between the SWF and the other state bodies, should be publicly disclosed. | CIC publicly discloses that its legal basis is in accordance with Company Law of the People's Republic of China. CIC does also disclose its legal relationship with its shareholder, the State Council, and its obligations to the Ministry of Finance and People's Bank of China. |
| GAPP 2 | The policy purpose of the SWF should be clearly defined and publicly disclosed. | CIC publicly discloses its policy purpose in its company profile. As stated in the *2011 Annual Report* overview, "It [CIC] was established as a vehicle to diversify China's foreign exchange holdings and achieve higher long-term returns within acceptable risk tolerance on its investments." |
| GAPP 4 | GAPP 4.1 Subprinciple: The source of SWF funding should be publicly disclosed. | The CIC website states that registration capital was funded from an "issuance of special bonds worth RMB 1.55 trillion by the Ministry of |

**Table A-9. (Continued)**

| GAPP | Principle/Subprinciple | Adherence |
|---|---|---|
| | | Finance." A subsequent capital injection of $30 billion from SAFE is also noted in the *2011Annual Report*. |
| | GAPP 4.2 Subprinciple: The general approach to withdrawals from the SWF and spending on behalf of the government should be publicly disclosed. | CIC does not state its approach to withdrawals. However, given the nature of the fund, withdrawals to supplement the national budget have not occurred. |
| GAPP 16 | The governance framework and objectives, as well as the manner in which the SWF's management is operationally independent from the owner, should be publicly disclosed. | Government framework and objectives are outlined in the "Corporate Governance" section of the *2011 AnnualRreport*. |
| GAPP 17 | Relevant financial information regarding the SWF should be publicly disclosed to demonstrate its economic and financial orientation, so as to contribute to stability in international financial markets and enhance trust in recipient countries. | CIC discloses relevant financial information such as asset allocation and the rate of return of its overseas portfolio. However, exact returns from its domestic portfolio, which includes Central Huijin, are undisclosed. |
| GAPP 18 | GAPP 18.3 Subprinciple: A description of the investment policy of the SWF should be publicly disclosed. | CIC does include a description of their investment policy that includes statements regarding its investment themes, objectives, horizon, and asset allocation in its annual report. |
| GAPP 19 | GAPP 19.1 Subprinciple: If investment decisions are subject to other than economic and financial considerations, these should be clearly set out in the investment policy and be publicly disclosed. | CIC's annual report discusses the investment decision process that is conducted under the CIC charter. All decision- making is conducted under the Investment Committee's oversight, which is then reviewed by the Investment Review Committee. CIC states that "CIC has full operational independence and makes its investment decisions based on its assessment of economic and financial objectives." |
| GAPP 21 | SWFs view shareholder ownership rights as a fundamental element of their equity investments' value. If an SWF chooses to exercise its ownership rights, it should do so in a manner that is consistent with its investment policy and protects the financial value of its investments. The SWF should publicly disclose its general approach to voting securities of listed entities, including the key factors guiding its exercise of ownership rights. | CIC states in its *2011 Annual Report*, "As a financial investor, we usually maintain a minority shareholder status and do not seek to control or influence investee companies. Nor do we always exercise our full ownership rights. When we do, we are consistent with our investment policy to protect the value of our investment. CIC continues to strengthen its post investment management process and strives to do what we can as a minority shareholder to help our investee companies achieve success. By helping these companies thrive, we also fulfill our own value creation objectives." |
| GAPP 22 | GAPP 22.2 Subprinciple: The general approach to the SWF's risk management framework should be publicly disclosed. | CIC discloses its risk management framework in its annual report. |

## Table A-10. CIC Financials, 2008-11

| **Consolidated Balance Sheets ($ millions)** | | | | |
|---|---|---|---|---|
| **Assets** | **2008** | **2009** | **2010** | **2011** |
| Cash and deposits | 47,803 | 18,622 | 14,480 | 20,088 |
| Financial assets at fair value through profit or loss | | | | |
| Cash and deposits | 45,436 | 20,673 | 3,458 | 8,058 |
| Equities | 1,949 | 39,828 | 65,645 | 59,718 |
| Fixed-income securities | 8,312 | 25,383 | 34,932 | 38,644 |
| Alternative investments | 362 | 7,430 | 29,274 | 40,470 |
| **Total financial assets at fair value through profit or loss** | 56,059 | 93,314 | 133,309 | 146,890 |
| Receivable and prepayments | 1,565 | 3,067 | 4,210 | 5,923 |
| Available-for-sale investments | N/A | N/A | 113 | 119 |
| Held-to-maturity investments | 15,189 | 14,424 | 2,000 | 2,000 |
| Long-term equity investments* | 171,156 | 201,409 | 253,340 | 304,880 |
| Deferred tax assets | 1,765 | 962 | 1,046 | 1,742 |
| Other assets | 4,003 | 596 | 1,081 | 525 |
| **Total Assets** | 297,540 | 332,394 | 409,176 | 482,167 |
| **CIC Liabilities ($ millions)** | | | | |
| | **2008** | **2009** | **2010** | **2011** |
| Financial liabilities at fair value through profit or loss | 5,346 | 4,057 | 2,637 | 494 |
| Bonds payable | N/A | N/A | 16,609 | 17,461 |
| Deferred tax liabilities | 43 | 1,575 | 3,772 | 1,505 |
| Other liabilities | 3,395 | 6,752 | 12,259 | 37,615 |
| **Total liabilities** | 8,784 | 12,384 | 35,277 | 57,072 |
| **Owner's Equity** | | | | |
| Owner's Capital | 200,000 | 200,000 | 200,000 | 200,000 |
| Capital reserves and others | 88,756 | 120,010 | 174,302 | 225,095 |
| Total owner's equity | 288,756 | 320,010 | 374,302 | 425,095 |
| Total liabilities and owner's equity | 297,540 | 332,394 | 409,579 | 482,167 |
| **Consolidated Income Statements ($ millions)** | | | | |
| **Investment income** | **2008** | **2009** | **2010** | **2011** |
| Interest income | 4,066 | 1,656 | 2,052 | 2,293 |
| Dividend income | 135 | 983 | 1,109 | 1,525 |
| Realized gains on investments | 50 | 186 | 1,838 | 2,621 |
| Unrealized gains (losses) from changes in fair value of investments | -6,495 | 10,318 | 9,784 | -11,350 |
| Investment income from long-term equity investments | 26,367 | 31,706 | 40,761 | 53,383 |
| Foreign exchange gains (losses) | -167 | 72 | -175 | 70 |
| Other income | N/A | N/A | 24 | 47 |
| **Total investment income** | 23,956 | 44,876 | 55,393 | 48,589 |

* Principally investments by Central Huijin.

**Table A-10. (Continued)**

| Expense | | | | |
|---|---|---|---|---|
| Investment expense | -42 | -106 | -311 | -385 |
| General and administrative expense | -32 | -47 | -79 | -135 |
| Finance expense | N/A | N/A | -213 | -660 |
| Impairment loss | -21 | N/A | 12 | N/A |
| **Total expense** | -95 | -153 | -591 | -1,180 |
| **Income** | | | | |
| **Operating income** | 23,861 | 44,723 | 54,802 | 47,409 |
| Others, net | 1 | -25 | -1 | -2 |
| **Income before taxes** | 23,862 | 44,698 | 54,801 | 47,407 |
| Income taxes | -731 | -3,038 | -3,241 | 1,015 |
| **Net income** | 23,131 | 41,660 | 51,560 | 48,422 |

Source: China Investment Corporation, *2008-2011 Annual Reports* (Beijing, China).

## End Notes

[1] U.S. Economic and Ssecurity Review Commission (USCC), *2008 Report to Congress* (Washington, DC: U.S. Government Printing Office, November 2008), p.4.

[2] The City-UK estimates. http://stagingtcuk.positive-technology.com/research/our-work/reports-list/fund-management-2010/; Sovereign Wealth Fund Institute.

[3] Ashby Monk, “Recasting the Sovereign Wealth Fund Debate: Trust, Legitimacy, and Governance,” *New Political Economy* 14:4 (December 2009): 454; Guo Li, “Demystifying the Chinese Sovereign Wealth Fund – A Perspective of the U.S. Financial Regulation,” *Tsinghua China Law Review* 2:353 (April 2012): 9. http://tsinghuachinalawreview.org/articles/PDF/TCLR_0202_Guo.pdf.

[4] Dani Rodrik, “The Social Cost of Foreign Exchange Reserves,” *International Economic Journal* 20:3 (2006): 254-56.

[5] The Sovereign Wealth Fund Initiative, “A Conversation with Ted Truman, Senior Fellow, Peterson Institute for International Economics,” March 2012, p. 1. http://fletcher.tufts.edu/SWFI/~/media/Fletcher/Microsites/swfi/pdfs/2012/Truman%20Iview%20Final.pdf.

[6] Stephen Thomas and Ji Chen, "China's Sovereign Wealth Funds: Origins, Development, and Future Roles," *Journal of Contemporary China* 20:70 (2011): 472-73.

[7] Guo Li, “Demystifying the Chinese Sovereign Wealth Fund – A Perspective of the U.S. Financial Regulation,” *Tsinghua China Law Review* 2:353 (April 2012): 9. http://tsinghuachinalawreview.org/articles/PDF/TCLR_0202_Guo.pdf.

[8] World Bank data. http://data.worldbank.org/indicator/NY.GDP.PCAP.CD.

[9] Sarah Eaton and Zhang Ming, “A Principal-Agent Analysis of China’s Sovereign Wealth System: Byzantine by Design,” *Review of International Political Economy* 17:3 (2010): 492-94; Ming Zhang and Fan He, “China’s Sovereign Wealth Fund: Weakness and Challenges,” *China and World Economy* 17:1 (2009): 102-03.

[10] Stephen Thomas and Ji Chen, "China's Sovereign Wealth Funds: Origins, Development, and Future Roles," *Journal of Contemporary China* 20:70 (2011): 477.

[11] Sarah Eaton and Zhang Ming, “A Principal-Agent Analysis of China’s Sovereign Wealth System: Byzantine by Design,” *Review of International Political Economy* 17:3 (2010): 492-94; Ming Zhang and Fan He, “China’s Sovereign Wealth Fund: Weakness and Challenges,” *China and World Economy* 17:1 (2009): 102-03.

[12] Eiichi Sekine, "China's Foreign Exchange Reserves and China Investment Corporation's Steps towards Diversifying How It Manages Its Portion of Them," *Nomura Journal of Capital Markets* 1:4 (Winter 2009): 4; Jamil Anderlini, "China Investment Arm Emerges from Shadows," *Financial Times*, January 5, 2008; and Sarah Eaton and Zhang Ming, "A Principal-Agent Analysis of China's Sovereign Wealth System: Byzantine by Design," *Review of International Political Economy* 17:3 (2010): 492-94.

[13] Victor Shih, "Tools of Survival: Sovereign Wealth Funds in Singapore and China," *Geopolitics* 14:2 (2009): 336-37.

[14] Chris Wright, "China's CIC: Change of the Guard," *Financial Times*, May 13, 2013. http://blogs.ft.com/beyond-brics/2013/05/13/chinas-cic-change-of-the-guard/?#.

[15] Sarah Eaton and Zhang Ming, "A Principal-Agent Analysis of China's Sovereign Wealth System: Byzantine by Design," *Review of International Political Economy* 17:3 (2010): 492-94.

[16] International Working Group of Sovereign Wealth Funds, "Sovereign Wealth Funds Current Institutional and Operational Practices,", September 15, 2008. http://www.iwg-swf.org/pubs/eng/swfsurvey.pdf; Christopher Balding, "Who's Afraid of Sovereign Wealth Funds?" *Revue d'Economie Financiere* 9:1 (1997): 207-08; and Ming Zhang and Fan He, "China's Sovereign Wealth Fund: Weakness and Challenges," *China and World Economy* 17:1 (2009): 107.

[17] The Central People's Government of the People's Republic of China, *Law of the People's Republic of China on the People's Bank of China* [Zhongguo Renmin Gonghe Guo Renmin Yinhang Fa]. http://www.gov.cn/test/2005-06/28/content_10577.htm.

[18] *Wall Street Journal*, "Q&A: China Investment Corporation's Wang Jianxi," March 6, 2012. http://blogs.wsj.com/chinarealtime/2012/03/06/qa-china-investment-corp-s-wang-jianxi/.

[19] Xinhua, "[CIC's Second Capitalization Study: MOF Issuance of Debt Method Superior], Zhongtou zai Zhuzi Diaocha: Caizhengbu Fazhai Fangan Zhanyou," August 10, 2011. http://finance.people.com.cn/h/2011/0810/c227865-1090121043.html.

[20] *Economic Observer,* "Plan to Split CIC Approved,", November 7, 2011. http://www.eeo.com.cn/ens/.2011/1107/215185.shtml; *Caixin*, "CIC to Receive a Stable Funding Mechanism [Zhongtou jiang huo wending zhuzi jizhi]," May 14, 2011. http://magazine.caixin.com/2011-05-14/100259166.html; and Xinhua, "CIC's Second Capitalization Study: MOF Issuance of Debt Method Superior [Zhongtou zai zhuzi diaocha: caizhengbu fazhai fanganzhanyou],", August10, 2011. http://finance.people.com.cn/h/2011/0810/c227865-1090121043.html.

[21] Yann Marin, "Chinese Sovereign Wealth Funds: Past, Present, and Future," *Revue d'Economie Financiere* 9:1(2009): 112.

[22] Patrick J. Schena, "The China Investment Corporation at 4 Years: An Evolving Legacy of Capitalization and Control," The Sovereign Wealth Fund Initiative, March 2012: p. 2.

[23] Stephen Thomas and Ji Chen, "China's Sovereign Wealth Funds: Origins, Development, and Future Roles," *Journal of Contemporary China* 20:70 (2011): 473-74.

[24] Caixin, "CIC to Receive a Stable Funding Mechanism [Zhongtou jiang huo wending zhuzi jizhi]," May 14, 2011. http://magazine.caixin.com/2011-05-14/100259166.html.

[25] *Yann Marin, "Chinese Sovereign Wealth Funds: Past, Present, and Future," Revue d'Economie Financiere* 9:1(2009): 110; Ming Zhang and Fan He, "China's Sovereign Wealth Fund: Weakness and Challenges," *China and World Economy* 17:1 (2009): 107; and Li Qing, "China's Sovereign Wealth Fund Faces Old Questions," *MarketWatch*, August 3, 2011, via Factiva.

[25] China Investment Corporation, *Annual Report 2010* (Beijing: July 2011), p.7.

[27] Eiichi Sekine, "China's Foreign Exchange Reserves and China Investment Corporation's Steps towards Diversifying How It Manages Its Portion of Them," *Nomura Journal of Capital Markets* 1:4 (Winter 2009): 7-8.

[28] Guo Li, "Demystifying the Chinese Sovereign Wealth Fund – A Perspective of the U.S. Financial Regulation," *Tsinghua China Law Review* 2:353 (April 2012): 12.

[29] Guo Li, "Demystifying the Chinese Sovereign Wealth Fund – A Perspective of the U.S. Financial Regulation," *Tsinghua China Law Review* 2:353 (April 2012): 12. http://tsinghuachinala wreview.org/articles/PDF/ TCLR_0202_Guo.pdf.

[30] Eiichi Sekine, "China's Foreign Exchange Reserves and China Investment Corporation's Steps towards Diversifying How It Manages Its Portion of Them," *Nomura Journal of Capital Markets* 1:4 (Winter 2009): 9.

[31] China Investment Corporation, *Annual Report 2011* (Beijing,China: July 2012), p. 4.

[32] Robert C. Pozen and Gu Xiaoyu, "Two Key Decisions for China's Sovereign Fund," Harvard Business School Case 311-337 (September 2011): 5-6.

[33] China Investment Corporation, *Annual Report 2011* (Beijing, China: July 2012), p. 7.

[34] *China Business Times*, "Who Will Take Responsibility for CIC's Continual Losses? [Zhongtou luzhanlubai shei lai wenze]," September 10, 2010. http://finance.sina.com.cn/roll/20100910/00013449600.shtml.

[35] Dow Jones International News, "China NPC: SAFE: Undecided on CIC Funding, to Grow Private Investment," March 8, 2010, via Factiva.

[36] China Investment Corporation annual reports, 2009 and 2010 (Beijing, China).

[37] Simon Rabinovitch, "China Fund Loses 4.3% in Global Portfolio," *Financial Times*, July 25, 2012, via Factiva.

[38] Eiichi Sekine, "China's Foreign Exchange Reserves and China Investment Corporation's Steps towards Diversifying How It Manages Its Portion of Them," *Nomura Journal of Capital Markets* 1:4 (Winter 2009): 10.

[39] Thao Hua, "Chinese Giant to Outsource Billions," *Pensions and Investments* 38:17 (August 23, 2010), via Factiva.

[40] Dai Tian, "CIC Eyes More Investments in Manufacturing, Property," *Caixin*, January 15, 2013, via Factiva.

[41] "CIC Invests in Carlyle's Property in Manhattan," *China Knowledge Press*, January 4, 2011, via Factiva.

[42] China Investment Corporation, *Annual Report 2011* (Beijing, China: July 2012), p. 3; Nisha Gopalan, "At CIC, Resources Spell Pain," Dow Jones News Service, June 15, 2012. http://blogs.wsj.com/deals/2012/06/13/at-cic-resources-spell-pain/.

[43] Mary Lee, "China Investment Corp Walks Away from Pantheon Ventures," *Greater China Private Equity Review Daily*, October 12, 2010, via Factiva.

[44] China Investment Corporation annual reports, 2008-2011 (Beijing, China).

[45] Eric Ng, "State Fund Urges Washington to Ease Curbs," *South China Morning Post* (Hong Kong), January 21, 2010, via Factiva.

[46] *Financial Times,* "CIC launches Hong Kong subsidiary,", October 19, 2012. http://www.ft.com/intl/cms/s/0/90f5bb38-dba0-11df-a1df-00144feabdc0.html#axzz2RDc9aTvp.

[47] China Investment Corporation, 2010 *Annual Report* 2010 (Beijing, China: July 2011), p. 6.

[48] China Investment Corporation annual reports, 2010-2011 (Beijing, China).

[49] Brad Setser, "The China-Once-Again-Investing Corporation," (New York, NY: Council on Foreign Relations, June 10, 2009). http://blogs.cfr.org/setser/2009/06/10/the-china-once-again-investing-corporation/.

[50] Christopher Balding, "Who's Afraid of Sovereign Wealth Funds?" *Revue d'Economie Financiere* 9:1 (1997): 203; Dinny McMahon and Wei Lingling, "China Quietly Invests Reserves in U.K. Properties," *Wall Street Journal*, February 24, 2013. http://online.wsj.com/article/SB10001424127887323699704578323670119279066.html.http://online.wsj.com/article/SB10001424127887323699704578323670119279066.html?mg=id-wsj.

[51] Wei Lingling, "China Pension Fund Considering Investing In Foreign Private Equity – Sources," *Wall Street Journal*, January 6, 2012, via Factiva.

[52] Patrick J. Schena, "The China Investment Corporation at 4 Years: An Evolving Legacy of Capitalization and Control," The Sovereign Wealth Fund Initiative, March 2012 pp. 4-5.

[53] Sarah Eaton and Zhang Ming, "A Principal-Agent Analysis of China's Sovereign Wealth System: Byzantine by Design," *Review of International Political Economy* 17:3 (2010): 481.

[54] Patrick J. Schena, "The China Investment Corporation at 4 Years: An Evolving Legacy of Capitalization and Control," The Sovereign Wealth Fund Initiative, March 2012 p. 5.

[55] Dinny McMahon and Wei Lingling, "China Quietly Invests Reserves in U.K. Properties," *Wall Street Journal*, February 24, 2013. http://online.wsj.com/article/SB10001424127888732369 9704578323670119279066.html.

[56] Bloomberg, "China to Use Forex Reserves to Finance Overseas Investment Deals," January 14, 2013. http://www.bloomberg.com/news/2013-01-14/china-to-use-forex-reserves-to-finance-overseas-investment-deals.html.

[57] *Dow Jones Business News,* "China Pension Fund to Raise Foreign Investment to 20% of Assets,", December 16, 2009, via Factiva.

[58] Xinhua, "China's Social Security Fund to Expand to 300 Bln USD in 2015: Fund Chairman," April 11, 2010, via Factiva; James Anderlini, "Chinese Fund Eyes Expansion in the West," *Financial Times*, March 30, 2010, via Factiva.

[59] *Asia Private Equity Review*, "China's Institutional Investors Are Buying Home Assets," February 1, 2009, via Factiva.

[60] Dinny McMahon and Wei Lingling, "China Quietly Invests Reserves in U.K. Properties," *Wall Street Journal*, February 24, 2013. http://online.wsj.com/article/SB10001424127887323699 704578323670119279066.html.http://online.wsj.com/article/SB10001424127888732369970 4578323670119279066.html?mg=id-wsj.

[61] Spencer Anderson, "Sheer Size Requires a Degree of Discretion," *Financial Times*, February 22, 2010, via Factiva.

[62] Xinhua, "China's Pension Fund Unveils New Global Investment Managers," July 18, 2012, via Factiva.

[63] Wei Lingling, "China Pension Fund Considering Investing In Foreign Private Equity – Sources," *Wall Street Journal*, January 6, 2012, via Factiva.

[64] USCC, *2008 Report to Congress* (Washington, DC: U.S. Government Printing Office, 2008), p. 49.

[65] Bloomberg, "China Joining U.S. Shale Renaissance With $40 Billion," March 5, 2013. http://www.bloomberg.com/news/2013-03-05/china-joining-u-s-shale-renaissance-with-40-billion.html.

[66] International Energy Agency, "Overseas Investments by Chinese National Oil Companies" (Paris, France: February, 2011). http://www.iea.org/publications/freepublications/publication/overseas_china.pdf.

[67] Interfax, "Interfax Russia and CIS Energy Daily," October 16, 2009, via Factiva.

[68] *People's Daily*, "China's Largest Oil Producer to Lend $5 Bln to Kazakhstan for Oil Assets," April 17, 2009. http://english.people.com.cn/90001/90778/90857/90861/6639678.html.

[69] Central Intelligence Agency World Factbook,"Country Comparison: Natural Gas – Proved Reserves" (Langley, VA). https://www.cia.gov/library/publications/the-world-factbook/rankorder/2179rank.html.

[70] *Financial Times*, "CIC Buys Stake in Kazakh Oil and Gas Group," September 30, 2009. http://www.ft.com/intl/cms/s/0/be3bd146-ad88-11de-bb8a-00144feabdc0.html#axzz2RDc9aTvp.

[71] *Energy Daily,* "China Loans 10 Bln Dlrs to Kazahkstan: State Media,", April 17, 2009. http://www.energy-daily.com/reports/China_loans_10_bln_dlrs_to_Kazakhstan_state_media_999.html.

[72] *Energy Daily,* "China Loans 10 Bln Dlrs to Kazahkstan: State Media," April 17, 2009. http://www.energy-daily.com/reports/China_loans_10_bln_dlrs_to_Kazakhstan_state_media_999.html.

[73] *Forbes,* "What To Expect From A Sinopec-Chesapeake Deal," June 21, 2012. http://www.forbes.com/sites/christopherhelman/2012/06/21/what-to-expect-from-a-sinopec-

chesapeake-deal/; *Wall Street Journal,* "Sinopec to Buy Stake in Chesapeake Energy Asset,", February 25, 2013. http://online.wsj.com/article/SB10001424127887324338604578325901158645038.html; and Chesapeake Energy Corporation, "Chesapeake Energy Corporation Announces $1.02 Billion Mississippi Lime Joint Venture,", (Oklahoma City, OK: February 25, 2013). http://www.chk.com/news/articles/Pages/1788571.aspx.

[74] Cheniere Energy website, "Sabine Pass Liquefaction Project." http://www.cheniere.com/lng_industry/sabine_pass_liquefaction.shtml.

[75] *Guardian* (United Kingdom), "Chinese State Fund Buys 1.6% in Total," April 3, 2008. http://www.guardian.co.uk/business/2008/apr/04/oil.mergersandacquisitions.

[76] Total company website, "Activities in China.". http://www.cn.total.com/activities/gas_power.ip? locale=en.

[77] Kash Burchett, "Chinese Sovereign Wealth Fund Eyeing Repsol LNG Assets," *I H S Global Insight Daily Analysis*, December 20, 2012, via Factiva; *ENP Newswire,* "GDF Suez Reinforces Its Commitment to China and to the Asia-Pacific Region,", November 2, 2011, via Factiva; *Greater China Private Equity Review Daily,* "CIC Invests in EIG Global Energy Partners,", February 3, 2012, via Factiva.

[78] *Economist*, "The Lore of Iron Ore," October 13, 2012. http://www.economist.com/node/21564559.

[79] Kevin Jianjun Tu and Sabine Johnson-Reiser, "Understanding China's Rising Coal Imports" (Washington, DC: Carnegie Endowment for International Peace, February 16, 2012). http://carnegieendowment.org/2012/02/16/understanding-china-s-rising-coal-imports/9ooh.

[80] *Foreign Affairs* and International Trade Canada press release, "A Canadian Success Story: Teck Resources Opens New Office in China," April 16, 2013. http://www.international.gc.ca/media_commerce/release_photo_distribution/2013/04/16c.aspx?lang=engbusiness/ 2010-10/09/content_11388391.htm.

[81] *People's Daily*, "Teck May Reap Gains from CIC Alliance," December 2, 2009. http://english.peopledaily.com.cn/90001/90778/90861/6829599.html.

[82] *Foreign Affairs* and International Trade Canada press release, "A Canadian Success Story: Teck Resources Opens New Office in China," April 16, 2013. http://www.international.gc.ca/media_commerce/release_photo_distribution/2013/04/16c.aspx?lang=eng; *China Daily*, "CIC's Teck Holding Pays Big Dividends," October 9, 2010. http://www.chinadaily.com.cn/ business/2010-10/09/content_11388391.htm.

[83] *Wall Street Journal,* "Resource-Rich Canada Looks to China for Growth," May 13, 2012, via Factiva.

[84] "Ovoot Tolgoi," South Gobi Resources company website, http://www.southgobi.com/s/Home.asp.

[85] *Wall Street Journal,* "Bumi Resources Secures $600M Loan To Refinance Short-Term Debt," February 8, 2012. http://online.wsj.com/article/BT-CO-20120208-709347.html.

[86] China Investment Corporation, "China Investment Corporation Invests in PT Bumi Resources Tbk," (Beijing, China: November 5, 2009). http://www.china-inv.cn/cicen/resources/news_20091116_351541.html; *Jones Day, "PT Bumi Resources Closes Loan with China Investment Corporation,", September 2009.* http://www.jonesday.com/experiencepractices/ExperienceDetail.aspx?experienceid=24811.

[87] Bloomberg, "Bumi Resources Swings to $666.2 Million Net Loss on Coal Prices," April 2, 2009. http://www.bloomberg.com/news/2013-04-02/bumi-resources-swings-to-666-2-million-net-loss-on-coal- prices.html.

[88] *Wall Street Journal*, "Bumi Resources Secures $600M Loan To Refinance Short-Term Debt," February 8, 2012. http://online.wsj.com/article/BT-CO-20120208-709347.html; *Wall Street Journal*, "Bumi Resources Looks to Pay Off CIC Debt," August 31, 2012. http://online.wsj.com/article/SB10000872396390444914904577622782102196126.html.

[89] Daniel Haberly, "Strategic Sovereign Wealth Fund Investment and the New Alliance Capitalism: A Network Mapping Investigation," *Environment and Planning* 43 (2011): 1833-1852.

[90] David Barboza, "China Sentences Rio Tinto Employees in Bribe Case," *New York Times*, March 29, 2010. http://www.nytimes.com/2010/03/30/business/global/30riotinto.html?pagewanted=all&_r=0.

[91] Shanduka Group company website, "Investee Companies.". http://www.shanduka.co.za/investees/Shanduka-Coal/index.html.

[92] Duke Energy Corporation, "Duke Energy Signs MOU with China Huaneng Group to Pursue Renewable and Other Clean-Energy Technologies," April 10, 2009. http://www.duke-energy.com/news/releases/2009081001.asp.

[93] AES Gener S.A., "AES Global Presence," March 2011. http://www.aesgener.cl/AESGenerWebNeo/Controls/Neochannels/Neo_CH6175/deploy/AES%20Gener%20March%202011.pdf.

[94] Jeffrey Ryser, "AES Plans to Sell 15 Percent of Company Stock to Chinese State-Owned Group for $1.58 Bil," *Global Power Report*, November 12, 2009, via Factiva.

[95] *MarketWatch*, "AES Getting $2 Billion from China Sovereign Fund; Adjusted Earnings Fall on Lower Revenue," November 6, 2009, via Factiva.

[96] *MarketWatch*, "AES Getting $2 Billion from China Sovereign Fund; Adjusted Earnings Fall on Lower Revenue," November 6, 2009, via Factiva.

[97] Steven Mufson, "Chinese Company to Buy a Stake in AES; Arlington Firm Seeks Money for New Projects, Ties to Asia," *Washington Post*, November 7, 2009, via Factiva.

[98] Wan Xu and Don Durfee, "China's State Grid in Talks to Buy AES' U.S. Wind Assets – Sources," Reuters, February 27, 2012, via Factiva.

[99] Global Logistic Properties press release, "GLP Expands Global Platform to Brazil; Establishes Market- Leading Presence with Significant Growth Opportunities," November 14, 2012. http://www.glprop.com/pressReleases_detail.php?news_id=97; Bloomberg, "Global Logistic, CIC to Buy $1.6 Billion of Japan Warehouses," December 20, 2011. http://www.bloomberg.com/news/2011-12-19/global-logistic-cic-to-buy-1-6-billion-of-japanese-assets-from-lasalle.html.

[100] Victor Shih, "Tools of Survival: Sovereign Wealth Funds in Singapore and China," *Geopolitics* 14:2 (2009): 328-344.

[101] USCC, *2008 Report to Congress* (Washington, DC: U.S. Government Printing Office, 2008), p. 49.

[102] *Wall Street Journal*, "Resource-Rich Canada Looks to China for Growth," May 13, 2012, via Factiva.

[103] *Entertainment Close-Up*, "AES Board of Directors Names Zhang Guobao to Board," December 14, 2011, via Factiva.

[104] CICC company website, "CICC Shareholders.". http://www.cicc.com/CICC/english/about/page2.htm.

[105] Victor Shih, "Tools of Survival: Sovereign Wealth Funds in Singapore and China," *Geopolitics* 14:2 (2009): 339.

[106] Reuters, "KIC, CIC, Temasek to Invest in Chesapeake Stake," June 21, 2010. http://www.reuters.com/article/2010/06/21/kic-korea-us-idUSTOE65K06920100621.

[107] Reuters, "CIC, GIC Jointly Invest $1 billion in U.S. Cheniere's LNG Plant: Source," August 20, 2012. http://www.reuters.com/article/2012/08/21/us-cic-cheniere-idUSBRE87K03D20120821.

[108] *Financial News*, "Mind the Gap: Asian Sovereign Wealth Funds Step into the Breach; Balance of Investor Power in Private Equity Shifts," November 28, 2011, via Factiva.

[109] Brian Spegele, "World News: China to Invest In Russian Fund," *Wall Street Journal,* October 12, 2011, via Factiva; Li Jing, "CIC to Invest in Russian Fund," *Caixin* online, October 12, 2011, via Factiva.

[110] Interfax and *CIS Business and Investment Weekly*, "Russia-China Fund Plans Timber Investment," September 7, 2012, via Factiva; Cao Wenjiao, "China, Russia Launch Joint Investment Fund," *Caixin* online, June 6, 2012, via Factiva.

[111] *Private Equity Asia*, "Russia-China $2bn Fund Eyes Commodities, Infra,"July 9, 2012, via Factiva.

[112] Chris Wright, "China's CIC and the Moscow Exchange: Benign Bonhomie?" *Financial Times*, February 15, 2013. http://blogs.ft.com/beyond-brics/2013/02/15/chinas-cic-and-the-moscow-exchange-benign-bonhomie/?Authorised=false#axzz2VT6fYDZI.

[113] *Wall Street Journal,* "CIC Invested about $2 Billion in Alibaba," September 19, 2012. http://online.wsj.com/article/SB10000872396390444620104 57800.6090686413784.html; *Caijing*, "Huijin to Buy 38per cent of New China Life Insurance," March 30, 2009. http://english.caijing.com.cn/2009-03-30/110130267.html.

[114] "CIC to buy stake in HK rail group float," Financial Times, November 21, 2007. http://www.ft.com/intl/cms/s/0/db127dc0-978b-11dc-9e08-0000779fd2ac.html#axzz2VpKo Skev; "CIC Is Said to Buy $400 Million Longyuan IPO Shares," Bloomberg, November 23, 2009. http://www.bloomberg.com/apps/news?pid=newsarchive&sid=ay4ghyHsK93g; "China Sovereign Fund Buys $710 Million GCL-Poly Stake," Bloomberg, November 19, 2009. http://www.bloomberg.com/apps/news?pid=newsarchive&sid=abXEKwLZIeno; "A Close Look at CIC's Recent Investments," Economic Observer, March 30, 2010. http://www.eeo.com.cn/ens/finance_investment/2010/03/30/166470.shtml; "SMIC to Receive Investment from CIC," Semiconductor Manufacturing International Corporation (SMIC) website, http://www.smics.com/eng/press/press_releases_details.php?id=59930.

[115] *Shanghai Daily*, "CIC Stake Buy Shows Focused Investment," November 20, 2009, via Factiva.

[116] Jackie Cheung, "China Sovereign Fund Buys Poly Hong Kong Stake, Property Company Says CIC Intends Long-Term Investment," *Wall Street Journal*, September 21, 2009, via Factiva.

[117] International Working Group of Sovereign Wealth Funds, *Generally Accepted Principles and Practices (GAPP) – Santiago Principles.* http://www.iwg-swf.org/pubs/gapplist.htm.

[118] Sarah Bagnall and Edwin M. Truman, "IFSWF Report on Compliance with the Santiago Principles:Admirable but Flawed Transparency," (Washington, DC: Peterson Institute for International Economics Policy Brief 11-14 (August 2011). http://www.iie.com/publications/pb/pb11-14.pdf.

[119] Xinhua *Financial Network*, "China Investment Corp Pledges Transparency, Opposes IMF Code of Conduct,", April 6, 2008, via Factiva.

[120] Daniel W. Drezner, "Bad Debts: Assessing China's Financial Influence in Great Power Politics," *International Security* 34:2 (Fall 2009): 28-31.

[121] China Investment Corporation, *2008 Annual Report,* (Beijing, China: August 2009), p. 16.

[122] Eiichi Sekine, "China Investment Corporation: Investment Performance in 2010 and Outlook," *Nomura Journal of Capital Markets* 3:3 (Winter 2012): 11.

[123] *Wall Street Journal*, "Overheard: Not-So-Great Leap," July 27, 2011, via Factiva.

[124] Eiichi Sekine, "China's Foreign Exchange Reserves and China Investment Corporation's Steps towards Diversifying How It Manages Its Portion of Them," *Nomura Journal of Capital Markets* 1:4 (Winter 2009): 13.

[125] Christopher Balding, "Who's Afraid of Sovereign Wealth Funds?" *Revue d'Economie Financiere* 9:1 (1997): 207.

[126] China Investment Corporation, *2011 Annual Report* (Beijing, China: July 2012).

[127] Maggie Lee, "NSSF VP Transferred to CIC for Better Overseas Investments," *Greater China Private Equity Review Daily*, June 20, 2011, via Factiva.

[128] China Investment Corporation, *2011 Annual Report* (Beijing, China: July 2012).

[129] Christopher Balding, "Who's Afraid of Sovereign Wealth Funds?" *Revue d'Economie Financiere* 9:1 (1997): 207.

[130] Chris Wright, "China's CIC: Change of the Guard," *Financial Times*, May 13, 2013. http://blogs.ft.com/beyond-brics/2013/05/13/chinas-cic-change-of-the-guard/?#.

[131] *Financial Times*, "China Struggles to Find Head for CIC Sovereign Wealth Fund," May 26, 2013. http://www.ft.com/intl/cms/s/0/451808d0-c5ca-11e2-99d1-00144feab7de.html#axzz2 VSpWKXxA.

[132] George Chen, "SCMP: Power Struggle in Beijing Leave CIC Leaderless," *South China Morning Post* (Hong Kong), May 27, 2013. http://www.scmp.com/news/china/article/1246905/powerstruggle-beijing-leaves-cic-leaderless?utm_source=Sinocism+Newsletter&utm_campaign=342b9fadff-Sinocism05_28_13&utm_medium=email&utm_term=0_171f237867-342b9fadff-24564729.

[133] Larry Cata Backer, "Sovereign Investing in Times of Crisis: Global Regulation of Sovereign Wealth Funds, State Owned Enterprises and the Chinese Experience," *Transnational Law and Contemporary Problems* 19:1 (November 2009): 252-53.

[134] International Working Group of Sovereign Wealth Funds, "Sovereign Wealth Funds Generally Accepted Principles and Practices 'Santiago Principles,". http://www.iwg-swf.org/pubs/eng/santiagoprinciples.pdf.

[135] Norwegian Ministry of Finance website. "The Norwegian Government Pension Fund Global Adherence with the Santiago Principles." http://www.regjeringen.no/Upload/FIN/brosjyre/2011/GapSurvey_Global.pdf.

[136] International Working Group on Sovereign Wealth Funds.,"Member's Information." http://www.ifswf.org/members-info.htm#chi.

[137] National Audit Office, "Audit System in China.". http://www.cnao.gov.cn/main/AboutUs _ ArtID_727.htm.

[138] China Investment Corporation, *2011 Annual Report* (Beijing,China: July 2012), p. 14.

[139] Li Qing, "Closer Look: CIC's Central Huijin Screen," *Caixin* online, July 29, 2011, via Factiva.

[140] *Financial Times,* "Paper Trail Leads to London's Top Stocks," September 12, 2008, via Factiva.

[141] Dinny McMahon and Wei Lingling, "China Quietly Invests Reserves in U.K. Properties," *Wall Street Journal*, February 24, 2013. http://online.wsj.com/article/SB10001424127887323699704578323670119279066.html.http://online.wsj.com/article/SB10001424127887323699704578323670119279066.html?mg=id-wsj.

[142] *Sinocast China Financial Watch*, "SAFE Investment Said to Buy Stake in 3 Australian Banks," January 7, 2008, via Factiva.

[143] *Canberra Times* (Australia), "China Set to Pour in Billions to Australia," January 15, 2013, via Factiva.

[144] Christopher Balding, "Who's Afraid of Sovereign Wealth Funds?" *Revue d'Economie Financiere* 9:1 (2009), pp. 201-210.

[145] China Investment Corporation, *Annual Report 2011* (Beijing: July 201), p.28.

[146] Larry Cata Backer, "Sovereign Investing in Times of Crisis: Global Regulation of Sovereign Wealth Funds, State Owned Enterprises and the Chinese Experience," *Transnational Law and Contemporary Problems* 19:1 (November 2009): 273-89.

[147] *SinoCast Investment and Securities Beat*, "CIC Makes All-Around Investments in North America," June 10, 2010, via Factiva.

[148] U.S.-China Economic and Security Review Commission, *Hearing on the Implications of Sovereign Wealth Fund Investments for National Security*, testimony of Robert H. Smith, February 7, 2008.

[149] James K. Jackson, "The Exon-Florio National Security Test for Foreign Investment" (Washington, DC: Congressional Research Service, March 29, 2013 pp. 2-3.

[150] James K. Jackson, "The Exon-Florio National Security Test for Foreign Investment" (Washington, DC: U.S. Congressional Research Service, March 29, 2013), pp. 1-3; Committee on Foreign Investment in the United States, *Annual Report to Congress* (Washington, DC: December 2012).

[151] James K. Jackson, "The Exon-Florio National Security Test for Foreign Investment" (Washington, DC: U.S. Congressional Research Service, March 29, 2013), pp. 1-3; Committee on Foreign Investment in the United States, *Annual Report to Congress* (Washington, DC: December 2012).

152 *Inside US-China Trade*, "CFIUS Review Of 3Com Deal Seen As First Major Test Of Reform Law," January 16, 2008, via Factiva.

153 Sullivan & Cromwell LLP website. http://www.sullcrom.com/International-Trade-and-InvestmentCFIUS-Practices/.

154 Eric Ng, "State Fund Urges Washington to Ease Curbs," *South China Morning Post* (Hong Kong), January 21, 2010, via Factiva.

155 Covington and Burlington website. http://www.cov.com/dfagan/.

156 Securities and Exchange Commission, *Form 13F—Reports Filed by Institutional Investment Managers*. http://www.sec.gov/answers/form13f.htm.

157 *Wall Street Journal*, "CIC Offers a Glimpse Into U.S. Holdings," February 9, 2010. http://online.wsj.com/article/SB10001424052748703427704575052303975503216.html.

158 Securities and Exchange Commission, "China Investment Corp," *Next-Generation EDGAR System* (Washington, DC). http://www.sec.gov/cgi-bin/browse-edgar?action=getcompany &CIK=0001468702&type=&dateb=&owner=exclude&count=100.

159 Guo Li, "Demystifying the Chinese Sovereign Wealth Fund – A Perspective of the U.S. Financial Regulation," *Tsinghua China Law Review* 2:353 (April 19, 2012): 357-58.

160 Guo Li, "Demystifying the Chinese Sovereign Wealth Fund – A Perspective of the U.S. Financial Regulation," *Tsinghua China Law Review* 2:353 (April 19, 2012): 357.

161 Sean P. Mahoney and Eric S. Yoon, "Chinese Banks Controlled by Sovereign Wealth Funds Receive Key Approvals from Federal Reserve, Highlighting Treatment of Sovereign Wealth Funds Under US Banking Laws," *The Sovereign Wealth Fund Initiative* (Summer 2012): 1.

162 Robert C. Pozen and Gu Xiaoyu, "Two Key Decisions for China's Sovereign Fund," Harvard Business School Case 311-337 (September 2011): 7; Guo Li, "Demystifying the Chinese Sovereign Wealth Fund – A Perspective of the U.S. Financial Regulation," *Tsinghua China Law Review* 2:353 (April 19, 2012): 367.

163 Robert C. Pozen and Gu Xiaoyu, "Two Key Decisions for China's Sovereign Fund," Harvard Business School Case 311-337 (September 2011): 7; Sean P. Mahoney and Eric S. Yoon, "Chinese Banks Controlled by Sovereign Wealth Funds Receive Key Approvals from Federal Reserve, Highlighting Treatment of Sovereign Wealth Funds Under US Banking Laws," *The Sovereign Wealth Fund Initiative* (Summer 2012): 2; and Guo Li, "Demystifying the Chinese Sovereign Wealth Fund – A Perspective of the U.S. Financial Regulation," *Tsinghua China Law Review* 2:353 (April 19, 2012): 367.

164 Robert C. Pozen and Gu Xiaoyu, "Two Key Decisions for China's Sovereign Fund," Harvard Business School Case 311-337 (September 2011): 7.

165 Guo Li, "Demystifying the Chinese Sovereign Wealth Fund – A Perspective of the U.S. Financial Regulation," *Tsinghua China Law Review* 2:353 (April 2012): 12.

166 Sean P. Mahoney and Eric S. Yoon, "Chinese Banks Controlled by Sovereign Wealth Funds Receive Key Approvals from Federal Reserve, Highlighting Treatment of Sovereign Wealth Funds Under US Banking Laws," *The Sovereign Wealth Fund Initiative* (Summer 2012): 3.

167 Robert C. Pozen and Gu Xiaoyu, "Two Key Decisions for China's Sovereign Fund," Harvard Business School Case 311-337 (September 2011): 7; Guo Li, "Demystifying the Chinese Sovereign Wealth Fund – A Perspective of the U.S. Financial Regulation," *Tsinghua China Law Review* 2:353 (April 19, 2012): 360-62.

168 Robert C. Pozen and Gu Xiaoyu, "Two Key Decisions for China's Sovereign Fund," Harvard Business School Case 311-337 (September 2011): 6-7; Guo Li, "Demystifying the Chinese Sovereign Wealth Fund – A Perspective of the U.S. Financial Regulation," *Tsinghua China Law Review* 2:353 (April 19, 2012): 366-67.

169 U. S. Federal Reserve, *Order Approving Acquisition of an Interest in a Bank Holding Company*, (Washington, DC: August 31, 2010), pp. 1-2. http://www.federalreserve.gov/newsevents/press/orders/order20100831a1.pdf.

170 U. S. Federal Reserve, *Order Approving Acquisition of an Interest in a Bank Holding Company*, (Washington, DC: August 31, 2010), pp. 7-8. http://www.federalreserve.gov/newsevents/press/orders/order2010083 1a1.pdf.

[171] Sean P. Mahoney and Eric S. Yoon, "Chinese Banks Controlled by Sovereign Wealth Funds Receive Key Approvals from Federal Reserve, Highlighting Treatment of Sovereign Wealth Funds Under US Banking Laws," *The Sovereign Wealth Fund Initiative* (Summer 2012): 3.

[172] Internal Revenue Service, *Bulletin 2011-48* (Washington, DC: November 28, 2011). http://www.irs.gov/irb/2011-48_IRB/ar14.html; Joel D. Almquist et al., "Proposed Tax Regulations Protect U.S. Tax Exemption for Sovereign Wealth Investors," *K&L Gates Legal Insight* (November 10, 2011). http://fletcher.tufts.edu/SWFI/~/media/Fletcher/Microsites/CEME/pubs/pdfs/Holt_HedgeFundTaxAlert.pdf.

[173] Internal Revenue Service, *Bulletin 2011-48* (Washington,DC: November 28, 2011). http://www.irs.gov/irb/2011-48_IRB/ar14.html; *Joel D. Almquist et al., "Proposed Tax Regulations Protect U.S. Tax Exemption for Sovereign Wealth Investors," K&L Gates Legal Insight* (November 10, 2011). http://fletcher.tufts.edu/SWFI/~/media/Fletcher/Microsites/CEME/pubs/pdfs/Holt_HedgeFundTaxAlert.pdf.

[174] Larry Cata Backer, "Sovereign Investing in Times of Crisis: Global Regulation of Sovereign Wealth Funds, State Owned Enterprises and the Chinese Experience," *Transnational Law and Contemporary Problems* 19:1 (November 2009): 203-04.

[175] Internal Revenue Service, *Bulletin 2011-48* (Washington, DC:November 28, 2011)., http://www.irs.gov/irb/2011-48_IRB/ar14.html; Joel D. Almquist et al., "Proposed Tax Regulations Protect U.S. Tax Exemption for Sovereign Wealth Investors," K&L Gates Legal Insight (November 10, 2011). http://fletcher.tufts.edu/SWFI/~/media/Fletcher/Microsites/CEME/pubs/pdfs/Holt_HedgeFundTaxAlert.pdf.

[176] C. Fred Bergsten & Joseph E. Gagnon, "Currency Manipulation, the US Economy, and Global Economic Order," *The Peterson Institute for International Economics Policy* Brief 12-25 (December 2012). http://www.iie.com/publications/interstitial.cfm?ResearchID=2302.

[177] Fu Tiantian, "Legal Problems with China's Sovereign Wealth Fund and the Path to Improvement [Woguo zhuquan caifu jijin cunzai de falu wenti ji wanshan tujing]," *Times Finance* [Shidai Jinrong] 6 (2012): 53-54.

[178] USCC, *2012 Report to Congress: Executive Summary and Recommendations* (Washington, DC: U.S. Government Printing Office, November 2012), p. 23.

In: China Investment Corporation
Editor: Ines Hembrecht
ISBN: 978-1-62808-913-4


*Chapter 2*

# TESTIMONY OF THILO HANEMANN, RESEARCH DIRECTOR, RHODIUM GROUP LLC. HEARING ON "TRENDS AND IMPLICATIONS OF CHINESE INVESTMENT IN THE UNITED STATES"*

## PATTERNS OF CHINESE INVESTMENT IN THE UNITED STATES

Co-chairs, members of the Commission: thank you for the opportunity to testify today.

I am research director at Rhodium Group (RHG), a New York-based economic research firm supporting the investment management, strategic planning and policy needs of firms in the private and public sectors. My own research focuses on global cross-border investment flows and the implications of the rise of China, India and other emerging markets as global investors.

I have been closely following Chinese overseas investment for more than five years and have published several studies on the topic. I also manage a proprietary database tracking Chinese investments in the U.S., and I would like to offer some numbers from this dataset to help the Commission better understand the extent of Chinese firms' operations and investments in the United States and answer some of the questions laid out for this hearing.

* This is an edited, reformatted and augmented version of a testimony, presented May 9, 2013 before the U.S.-China Economic and Security Review Commission.

This written statement summarizes some of these numbers. Charts representing the data graphically can be found in the Appendix.

## 1. Data on Chinese Investment in the U.S.

Analyzing Chinese investment in the U.S. is challenging due to lack of reliable and timely data sources. Neither the U.S. Bureau of Economic Analysis (BEA) nor Chinese statistical agencies offer a detailed breakdown of bilateral international investment positions. A rough picture of China's investments in the U.S. can be drawn using the BEA's international transactions data and the U.S. Treasury's International Capital System (TIC). The latest available data points are summarized in Figure 1 in the Appendix. [1]

BEA's latest available statistics on direct investment - which is traditionally defined as long-term ownership of 10% or more voting shares - put China's FDI stock in the U.S. at $3.8 billion at year-end 2011. Another data set from the BEA that is compiled after the ultimate beneficiary owner (UBO) principle puts the stock of Chinese investment at $9.5 billion at year-end 2011 - an indication that the extensive use of offshore financial centers and tax havens makes it difficult for statistical agencies to accurately track Chinese FDI.

However, this is the latest available official data point, and it dates back 1.5 years. In addition to a significant time lag, official sources also do not provide detailed data on the distribution of those investments and important variables like ownership or employment, often for confidentiality reasons.

Seeking more accurate and timely data, researchers have developed alternative databases to capture Chinese capital outflows by collecting information from regulatory filings, media reports and commercial M&A databases. One such database is Rhodium Group's *China Investment Monitor* (CIM), which covers acquisitions and greenfield projects by Chinese-owned firms in the United States with a value of $1 million and higher. It only includes investments that qualify as direct investment, using the 10% ownership threshold. The CIM is not directly comparable to data sets compiled using the traditional balance of payments approach to collecting FDI data, as it neglects reverse flows and does not fully capture intra-company loans and other follow-up flows. However, the bottom-up approach overcomes many of the weaknesses of the traditional approach - such as the incomplete accounting for flows through offshore financial centers - and allows for a detailed, real-time assessment of Chinese investment flows and ownership in the United Sates.[2]

## 2. Annual Flows of Chinese FDI to the U.S.

The RHG China Investment Monitor (CIM) records 633 Chinese deals in the United States between 2000 and 2012, amounting to $23.1 billion. These 633 deals consist of 445 greenfield projects – factories, offices and other facilities built from scratch – and 188 acquisitions of existing companies and assets. Acquisitions account for 85% of total investment value ($19.6 billion) and greenfield projects for the remaining 15% ($3.5 billion).

The annual patterns (presented in Figure 2 in the Appendix) illustrate the recent growth spurt in inflows. Before 2008, Chinese FDI flows into the United States typically stood below $1 billion annually, with the singular exception of Lenovo's $1.75 billion acquisition of IBM's personal computer division in 2005. Since 2008, Chinese investment has gained momentum, growing to just under $2 billion in 2009 and $5.5 billion in 2010. In 2011 Chinese investment came in slightly lower at $4.7 billion, but reached a new record high of $6.7 billion in 2012. With announced deals worth more than $10 billion by the end of the first quarter, 2013 will likely be another record year for Chinese direct investment in the United States.[3]

Our numbers on Chinese FDI transactions are higher than the latest available official data but still just a small percentage of total FDI in the United States. A few large-scale transactions and alarming headlines have led to the impression that China is "buying up" America.[4] This is not the case. Using official BEA figures for total FDI inflows (since our data does not cover FDI from *other* countries into the United States), China's $6.7 billion accounted for less than 4% of total U.S. FDI inflows of $175 billion in 2012.[5] China also remains a small share (less than 1%) of total inward FDI stock in the United States of $3 trillion by the end of 2012.[6]

At the same time, it is important to note that China was one of the few bright spots in a deteriorating global FDI environment in 2012. Foreign direct investment into the United States dropped markedly during the 2008/2009 financial crisis and has never recovered to previous levels. In 2012, FDI inflows to the United States were down 25% compared to previous year, partially because European firms were investing less. The rapid increase of FDI from China goes against the global trend, highlighting China's potential to become a significant source of FDI for the U.S. in the future.

## 3. U.S. Industries Favored by Chinese Investors

The recent increase of Chinese FDI in the United States is driven by a mix of changing policy conditions and commercial motives. On the policy side, Beijing's official line flipped from opposed to highly supportive of FDI in overseas markets. This reversal was rooted in the interests of several bureaucracies, including awareness of the importance of global operations for firm competitiveness (MOFCOM and SASAC), fading concerns about maximizing foreign exchange reserves (MOF and PBOC), and increasing awareness of the strategic vulnerability entailed in a U.S. debt-heavy portfolio of external assets (NDRC, PBOC and others).

While the ODFI approval process is still burdensome for many firms, it has been significantly relaxed in recent years.

While policy liberalization was an important prerequisite for growing Chinese outward FDI, the most important drivers of outward investment are changes in China's domestic economy that are pushing Chinese firms to invest overseas. The distribution of Chinese investment by industry (as presented in Table 1 in the Appendix) underscores those changes. Before the mid-2000s, Chinese FDI into the U.S. mostly consisted of smaller-scale operations to facilitate trade in electronics and other consumer goods. Since then, a much broader set of motives drew Chinese firms to invest in the U.S. In 18 industries, we find more than $200 million in Chinese deals, of which about half are in industrial and half in service sectors.

The biggest recipient of Chinese FDI is the U.S. oil and gas industry. The unconventional energy boom has made the United States a prime frontier for global oil and gas investments, and is attracting Chinese firms eager to expand their overseas production bases and involvement in cutting-edge extraction techniques. The 2005 CNOOC-Unocal deal failure chilled Chinese enthusiasm about natural resource projects in the United States, but the boom in unconventional oil and gas extraction has revived interest in North American acquisitions, resulting in several larger-scale oil and gas plays since 2010 adding up to more than $5 billion.[7]

American technology and advanced manufacturing are also attracting Chinese investment, fueled by structural adjustment at home. Increasing competition, rising factor input costs (especially labor), environmental compliance and remediation costs, and local impediments to consolidation to achieve economies of scale have spelled the end of the old Chinese business model focused on domestic markets and exports. These operating realities are compelling Chinese firms to look at U.S. assets to increase their competiveness at home and preserve access to U.S. customers abroad. The growing number of investments in industrial machinery, electrical equipment and components, automotive, alternative energy, medical devices and communications equipment illustrates the strong desire to invest in technology, brands, human talent and other competitive assets.

A related trend is increasing investment in modern service operations such as research and development, customer service and retail. Those investments complement the acquisition of advanced manufacturing assets and allow Chinese firms to tap into the U.S. talent base and move closer to their U.S. customers.[8] In the last two years we also saw increasing interest in acquiring core service sector assets, as Chinese firms gear up to profit from a domestic service sector boom.[9] The most targeted sectors are software and IT, hospitality and financial services.

Finally, direct investment stakes are increasingly becoming part of the asset management strategies of Chinese individuals, firms and institutional investors. Traditionally, those investors have a mandated "home bias" and hold most of their assets in China. However, given the risks of an undiversified portfolio and the current uncertainties about the outlook for growth in China, those investors are increasingly looking to diversify their portfolio internationally. Safe haven economies with a sound legal system and property rights protection like the United States are naturally attractive for such flows. The drop in prices following the financial crisis has made U.S. residential and commercial real estate an attractive target for these investors.[10] Other industries that traditionally offer stable long-term returns such as utilities have also attracted significant Chinese interest.

## 4. Geographic Location of Chinese FDI in the U.S.

Unlike official FDI statistics, our dataset also provides a detailed breakdown of Chinese investment by state. Those data points (presented in Figure 3 in the Appendix) show that the recent increase in volume and scope of investment has brought Chinese firms to at least 43 of the 50 states. Mapping out Chinese investment flows by state reveals that Chinese money largely follows in the paths of other foreign investors, with traditionally strong economies on the east and west coasts being the top recipients of Chinese investment. California is by far the number one destination for Chinese investment by number of deals, with more than 170 transactions between 2000 and 2012, or roughly one-quarter of all Chinese direct investments in the United States. The other top recipient states by number of deals are New York, Texas, Illinois, and North Carolina. In terms of total investment value, New York, Texas, Illinois and Virginia are leading the pack, followed by California. States with industry clusters that are attractive for Chinese investors have also received significant capital inflows, for example Michigan, Illinois and Ohio (automotive) or Texas (oil and gas).

## 5. Profile of Chinese Investors in the U.S.

Finally, our micro dataset allows for an in-depth analysis of Chinese investors in the United States by ownership and other variables. The first important finding here is that the pool of Chinese firms operating in the U.S. reflects the diversity of ownership in corporate China, ranging from sovereign investment entities (such as China Investment Corporation) to central state-owned enterprises (e.g., Sinopec) to firms with hybrid ownership structures (e.g., Lenovo), and wholly privately-owned firms (e.g., Wanxiang). Table 2 in the Appendix presents an overview of firms of different ownership types and their share in total Chinese investment in the U.S. from 2000-2012.

China's sovereign investment entities are making significant portfolio investments in the United States but have traditionally kept a low profile when it comes to direct investment. China's primary sovereign wealth fund, the China Investment Corporation (CIC), is an active investor in the United States, but has only made one investment in the U.S. that meets the direct investment threshold.[11] However, there are several investments by Chinese companies in which CIC has a significant ownership stake, for example the big state-owned banks. Several other high-profile government-controlled entities such as the State Administration of Foreign Exchange (SAFE) and the National Social Security Fund (NSSF) have portfolio investment positions in the United States, but have not yet ventured into FDI stakes.

State-owned enterprises account for only 27% of transactions from 2000-2012 but for 63% of total investment value in the same period. This reflects the fact that those SOEs are dominating capital intensive industries in China, and they are the ones closing the larger-scale deals in the U.S. too, for example in the extractive industry. Within the group of state-owned firms, central SOEs account for the majority of deals (73%) and investment value (75%) while firms owned by provincial and municipal governments play a smaller role (26% of deals and 25% of deal value). Private firms - which we define as those having 80% or greater nongovernment ownership - account for the vast majority of transactions in the United States: 461 of 633 recorded investments between 2000 and 2012, or 73%. In terms of total investment value, private firms accounted for only 37% of total flows from 2000-2012 as they tended to invest in smaller and less capital-intensive projects than SOEs. However, private firms have lately been catching up with SOEs and are becoming an increasingly important driver of capital flows. They are now interested in medium and large-scale deals, not just the smaller transactions seen in the past, and they are increasingly capable of managing those investments. In the fifteen months from January 2012 to March 2013, private firms have spent as much money on FDI transactions in the U.S as in the eleven years before combined. In the same period, they accounted for 80% of transactions and close to 50% of total transaction value (as displayed in Figure 4 in the Appendix).

## 6. Employment Impacts of Chinese Investment in the United States

Our dataset also tracks the number of Americans employed by the subsidiaries of Chinese firms in the US. Chinese firms were negligible employers before 2008, with the exception of Lenovo's acquisition of IBM's personal computer division in 2005. Since 2009 the number or jobs provided has increased substantially on the back of greater annual investment flows and an increase in large-scale acquisitions. We find that the number of jobs provided by majority Chinese-owned subsidiaries has grown from fewer than 2,000 in 2000 to around 10,000 in 2007 and more than 30,000 at the end of 2012 (Figure 5 in the Appendix).

Our figures only refer to U.S. subsidiaries with a Chinese *majority* ownership, so they do not include employment provided by firms in which Chinese investors hold a minority interest. The latter account for more than 40% of the total value of investments in our database from 2000-2012, including shale gas assets by Devon Energy or Chesapeake Energy. If we added jobs at firms with Chinese minority equity stakes, our figure would be higher by several thousands. Nor do we include indirect job creation related to the construction of facilities or at suppliers, which can be sizable; Tianjin Pipe Corporation's (TPCO) new steel plant in Texas, for instance, is estimated to employ 1,000-2,000 construction workers. The most prominent greenfield investors are Wanxiang, which entered the U.S. market in 1994 and grew into a diversified business employing 6,000 Americans; Haier, which established its first production facility in South Carolina in the late 1990s and today employs about 350 people; Huawei, which employs around 1,500 people at its R&D centers in California, Texas and New Jersey and other U.S. facilities; and Sany, which runs a manufacturing facility employing more than 130 people in Georgia. Big manufacturing projects currently under construction include TPCO's steel pipe plant in Texas and a copper tube manufacturing facility by Golden Dragon in Alabama. The impacts that mergers and acquisitions have on jobs are less clear. M&A deals can be positive for local employment if the investor saves the target from bankruptcy or hires additional staff after the acquisition. But the impacts could also be negative if the post-merger integration or restructuring results in the downsizing of local employment, or if the investor chooses to extract valuable assets and shut down local operations completely. Reviewing the M&A transactions in our data set that gave Chinese investors majority control of a U.S. company, we find that the jobs impact is overwhelmingly positive. We see no evidence of systematic "asset stripping" behavior and find that most Chinese parent firms have maintained or added staff after acquiring companies in the United States.[12]

## DATA APPENDIX

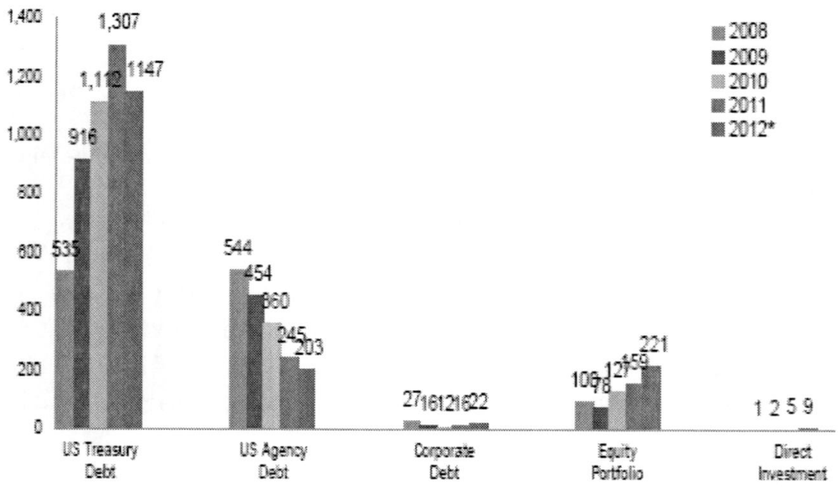


Sources: FDI figures based on ultimate beneficiary owner data from the Bureau of Economic Analysis; other figures from the U.S. Treasury International Capital System (TIC). *2012 data are preliminary estimates.

Figure 1. China's Investment Position in the United States, 2011/2012.

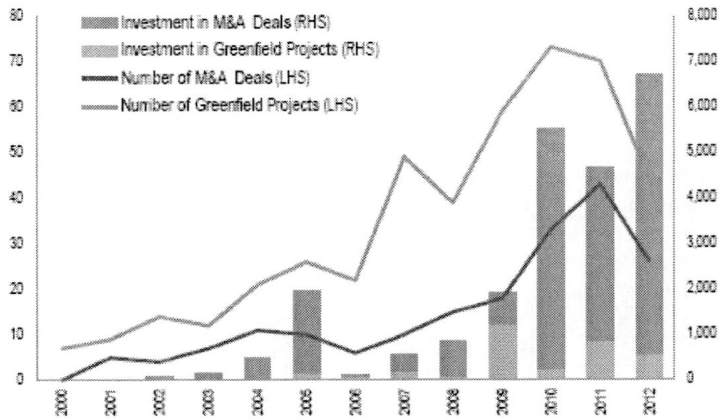


Source: Rhodium Group. *Numbers are preliminary and subject to adjustment. A detailed explanation of sources and methodology can be found at: http://rhg.com/interactive/china-investment-monitor.

Figure 2. Chinese Direct Investment in the United States, 2000-2012.* (Number of deals and USD million)

**Table 1. China's FDI in the U.S. by Industry, 2000-2012***
**USD million and number of deals**

| | | | Value (USD mn) | | | Number of Projects | | |
|---|---|---|---|---|---|---|---|---|
| | | | Greenfield | M&A | Total | Greenfield | M&A | Total |
| 1 | Coal, Oil and Gas | Primary | 6 | 5,250 | 5,255 | 4 | 11 | 15 |
| 2 | Farming, Logging and Husbandry | Primary | 15 | 64 | 79 | 1 | 7 | 8 |
| 3 | Paper, Rubber and other Materials | Primary | 111 | 0 | 111 | 15 | 0 | 15 |
| 4 | Aerospace Equipment and Components | Secondary | 106 | 460 | 566 | 4 | 5 | 9 |
| 5 | Automotive Equipment and Components | Secondary | 422 | 739 | 1,160 | 45 | 22 | 67 |
| 6 | Chemicals | Secondary | 5 | 4 | 9 | 5 | 1 | 6 |
| 7 | Consumer Products and Services | Secondary | 189 | 2,050 | 2,239 | 56 | 18 | 74 |
| 8 | Electronics and Electronic Parts | Secondary | 55 | 88 | 143 | 33 | 9 | 42 |
| 9 | Food Processing and Distribution | Secondary | 8 | 33 | 41 | 6 | 2 | 8 |
| 10 | Healthcare and Medical Devices | Secondary | 13 | 279 | 293 | 7 | 4 | 11 |
| 11 | Industrial Machinery and Tools | Secondary | 197 | 1,711 | 1,908 | 39 | 13 | 52 |

**Table 1. (Continued)**

| | | | Value (USD mn) | | | Number of Projects | | |
|---|---|---|---|---|---|---|---|---|
| | | | Greenfield | M&A | Total | Greenfield | M&A | Total |
| 12 | IT Equipment | Secondary | 221 | 190 | 411 | 36 | 6 | 42 |
| 13 | Metals and Minerals | Secondary | 1,256 | 70 | 1,327 | 14 | 4 | 18 |
| 14 | Other Transportation Equipment | Secondary | 51 | 5 | 55 | 9 | 1 | 10 |
| 15 | Pharmaceuticals and Biotechnology | Secondary | 65 | 192 | 257 | 20 | 6 | 26 |
| 16 | Renewable Energy | Secondary | 483 | 204 | 688 | 44 | 13 | 57 |
| 17 | Semiconductors | Secondary | 1 | 212 | 213 | 1 | 5 | 6 |
| 18 | Business Services | Tertiary | 43 | 318 | 361 | 20 | 15 | 35 |
| 19 | Construction Services | Tertiary | 6 | 0 | 6 | 4 | 0 | 4 |
| 20 | Entertainment, Media and Publishing | Tertiary | 9 | 2,614 | 2,623 | 4 | 5 | 9 |
| 21 | Financial Services and Insurance | Tertiary | 58 | 344 | 402 | 10 | 3 | 13 |
| 22 | Hospitality and Tourism | Tertiary | 13 | 345 | 358 | 1 | 5 | 6 |
| 23 | Real Estate | Tertiary | 0 | 992 | 992 | 0 | 10 | 10 |
| 24 | Software and IT Services | Tertiary | 176 | 612 | 788 | 45 | 21 | 66 |
| 25 | Transportation Services | Tertiary | 31 | 0 | 31 | 21 | 0 | 21 |
| 26 | Utilities | Tertiary | 1 | 2,813 | 2,814 | 1 | 2 | 3 |
| | Total | | 3,540 | 19,590 | 23,130 | 445 | 188 | 633 |

Source: Rhodium Group. *Numbers are preliminary and subject to adjustment. A detailed explanation of sources and methodology can be found at: http://rhg.com/interactive/china-investment-monitor.

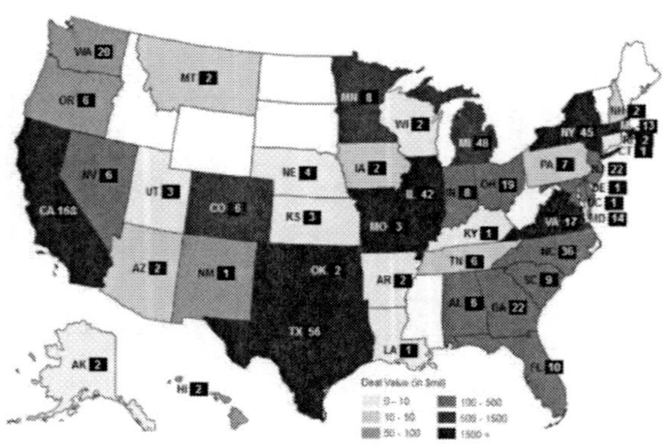


Source: Rhodium Group. *Numbers are preliminary and subject to adjustment. A detailed explanation of sources and methodology can be found at:http://rhg.com/interactive/china-investment-monitor.

Figure 3. Geographic Distribution of Chinese Direct Investment in the United States, 2000-2012.* (Accumulated deal value from 2000-2012, USD million)

**Table 2. China's FDI in the U.S. by Ownership of Investing Company, 2000-2012* USD million and number of deals**

| | | Number of Deals | | | | |
|---|---|---|---|---|---|---|
| | Greenfield | % share | M&A | % share | All Deals | % share |
| Government Controlled | 131 | 29% | 45 | 24% | 176 | 28% |
| Central SOEs | 84 | 19% | 23 | 12% | 107 | 17% |
| Provincial & Municipal SOEs | 29 | 7% | 16 | 9% | 45 | 7% |
| CIC & Central Huijin | 10 | 2% | 2 | 1% | 12 | 2% |
| Other | 8 | 2% | 4 | 2% | 12 | 2% |
| Private and Public* | 314 | 71% | 143 | 76% | 457 | 72% |
| | 445 | | 188 | | 633 | |
| | | Value of Deals | | | | |
| | Greenfield | % share | M&A | % share | All Deals | % share |
| Government Controlled | 2,227 | 63% | 12,399 | 63% | 14,626 | 63% |
| Central SOEs | 877 | 25% | 6,667 | 34% | 7,544 | 33% |
| Provincial & Municipal SOEs | 1,188 | 34% | 2,154 | 11% | 3,342 | 14% |
| CIC & Central Huijin | 49 | 1% | 1,721 | 9% | 1,770 | 8% |
| Other | 113 | 3% | 1,857 | 9% | 1,970 | 9% |
| Private and Public* | 1,313 | 37% | 7,191 | 37% | 8,504 | 37% |
| | 3,540 | | 19,590 | | 23,130 | |

Source: Rhodium Group.

*Numbers are preliminary and subject to adjustment. A detailed explanation of sources and methodology can be found at: http://rhg.com/interactive/china-investment-monitor;

**May include minority stakes by government-owned investors below a combined 20% of voting shares.

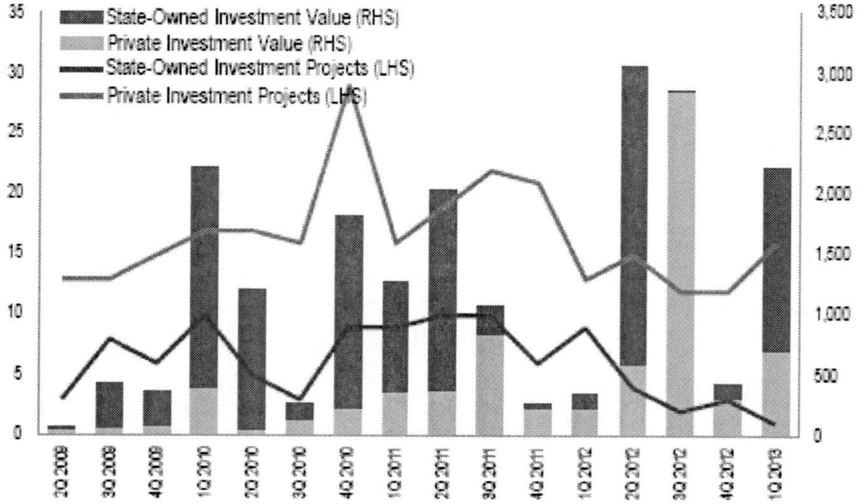


Source: Rhodium Group. *Numbers are preliminary and subject to adjustment. A detailed explanation of sources and methodology can be found at: http://rhg.com/interactive/china-investment-monitor.

Figure 4. Chinese Direct Investment in the US by Ownership, Q2 2009 – Q1 2013* (Quarterly figures, USD million)

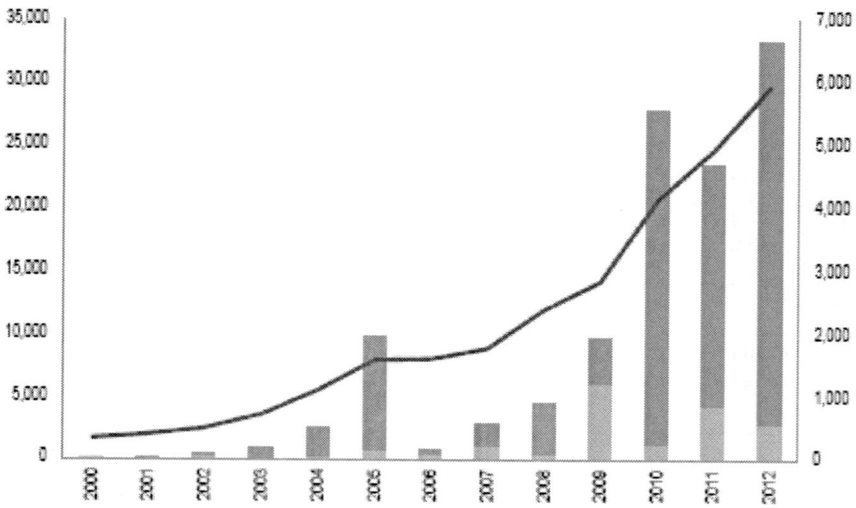


Source: Rhodium Group. *Numbers are preliminary and subject to adjustment. A detailed explanation of sources and methodology can be found at: http://rhg.com/interactive/china-investment-monitor.

Figure 5. Chinese FDI and Employment at Majority Chinese-Owned US Firms, 2000-2012.*

## End Notes

[1] These charts are the best available snapshots; they are by no means complete, as no reliable statistics exist due to difficulties capturing financial flows.

[2] For a detailed review of existing data sets and their advantages and weaknesses, see Rosen and Hanemann (2011) or Hanemann and Rosen (2012).

[3] See "Chinese FDI in the United States: Q1 2013 Update", Rhodium Group, http://rhg.com/notes/chinese-fdi-in-the-united- states-q1-2013-update

[4] See Time, "Will Asia "buy up" America?" August 30, 2011, available at: http://business.time.com/2011/08/30/will-asia-buy-up-america/.

[5] According to preliminary figures from the BEA, the U.S. registered $175 billion of inward direct investment flows in 2012.

[6] The BEA records an inward FDI stock of $3.07 trillion as of the end of 2012.

[7] For example, CNOOC's acquisition of stakes in Chesapeake Energy projects in 2010 and 2011 worth $1.7 billion and Sinopec's acquisition of Devon Energy in early 2012 valued at $2.5 billion.

[8] Some prominent examples include Huawei and Yingli Solar establishing high-tech R&D centers in California in 2011 and Lenovo establishing a fulfillment center in North Carolina in 2008.

[9] For example Wanda's acquisition of movie theater chain AMC in 2012.

[10] Both official statistics and our database underreport Chinese investment in U.S. real estate. However, recent examples of large- scale real estate grabs in the United States by Chinese firms include Shenzhen New World Group's dual acquisitions of Sheraton and Marriott hotels in Los Angeles in 2010 and 2011, and HNA Group's purchase of a New York City office building in 2011.

[11] This refers to CIC's 2010 $1.58 billion investment of Virginia's AES Corporation. Details of the deal can be found at: http://investor.aes.com/phoenix.zhtml?c=76149&p=irol-newsArticle&ID=1402516.

[12] For more details, see Rhodium Group, The Employment Impacts of Chinese Investment in the United States, http://rhg.com/articles/the-employment-impacts-of-chinese-invest ment- in-the-united-states.

In: China Investment Corporation
Editor: Ines Hembrecht
ISBN: 978-1-62808-913-4


*Chapter 3*

# TESTIMONY OF DEREK SCISSORS, SENIOR RESEARCH FELLOW IN ASIA ECONOMICS, THE HERITAGE FOUNDATION. HEARING ON "TRENDS AND IMPLICATIONS OF CHINESE INVESTMENT IN THE UNITED STATES"*

Now and for some time to come, the bulk of Chinese investment in the United States will take the form of Treasury bond holdings. Excluding bonds, Chinese investment in the U.S. is a $50 billion issue that could have been a $75 billion issue already and will be a $100 billion issue within a few years. When flowing out of an economy still largely centrally directed, this spending naturally raises questions about whether the investment strategy or strategies involved could harm American interests.

The answer is yes, but not to the extent and apparently not in the way some critics fear. There is plainly a strategic dimension to Chinese outward investment, and it has harmful elements. State-owned enterprises are instructed to acquire assets perceived as valuable by Beijing. They are heavily subsidized, posing questions about whether the clear benefits of investment in the U.S. are offset by anti-competitive influences. But these features are not hidden, much less insidious. Nor is Chinese strategy especially wise or effective.

* This is an edited, reformatted and augmented version of a testimony, presented May 9, 2013 before the U.S.-China Economic and Security Review Commission.

Unfortunately, this answer is incomplete. Indirect purchases by PRC entities do occur, as do clandestine attempts at technology acquisition. The U.S. should ask for voluntary disclosure of investments routed through third parties and sharpen disclosure requirements if the response is unsatisfactory. Dual-use technology should be protected by an enhanced Committee on Foreign Investment in the United States. To be genuinely productive, any steps the U.S. takes should themselves be transparent.

What American policymakers should avoid is discouraging Chinese investment on the basis of exaggerated hearsay. The facts on the ground indicate what are now well-known policy challenges and immediately useful steps to increase transparency. They do not come close to justifying protectionist actions.

## THE HERITAGE TRACKER

The Heritage Foundation's China Global Investment Tracker is the first public dataset in the field, including the limited offerings from the PRC government. It covers outward investment excluding bonds. The Tracker is global and extends back to 2005, the start of large-scale Chinese investment in the U.S. and the world. It utilizes corporate data and is updated semiannually.

The Tracker presently contains over 400 investment transactions of $100 million or more dated between January 1, 2005, and December 31, 2012. The total value of these transactions approaches $390 billion. The Tracker also contains an auxiliary dataset of over $200 billion worth of investments which have lost more than $100 million in value. Finally, it contains supplementary data on Chinese construction and engineering contracts worth well over $200 billion. (This list is incomplete and contains very few U.S. transactions to date.) [1]

The trend for Chinese outward, non-bond investment is to increase, if unsteadily. (See Appendix 1.) Investment in 2012 was close to $80 billion. Outbound investment will likely breach $100 billion annually by 2015 or 2016.

Official Chinese sector categories are topped in investment volume by "business and leasing services" and seem designed to draw attention away from an obvious bias to commodities. On the Heritage tally, energy is the top investment target. (See Appendix 2.) Within energy, oil leads but it is no longer dominant due to surging investment in integrated oil and gas projects. Metals is next; energy and metals together account for over 70 percent of Chinese outward investment since 2005. The heyday for finance was before the global crisis. Agriculture, real estate, and technology are other areas of high interest, while transportation is an area of high expertise.

Official Chinese data purport that Hong Kong receives at least 40 percent of annual investment and sometimes a good deal more. In fact, this money moves through Hong Kong on its way elsewhere. According to the Heritage tracker, the U.S. has pulled essentially even with Australia in the total amount of non-bond investment received since 2005. In 2012 alone, Canada led, via a $15 billion energy acquisition. Unsurprisingly, the European Union as a whole receives more than any individual country, though it is often the case that acquisitions are of European-headquartered companies and the bulk of the actual assets is located elsewhere.

Chinese firms have moved overseas in packs. Australia was the first destination, followed by sub-Saharan Africa, South America and, beginning in 2012, North America. It may be that the end of 2013 and start of 2014 will see another shift, perhaps to the oil-producing states in West Asia or assets physically located in Europe.

## U.S. Facts

The Tracker includes 58 Chinese investments of $100 million or more in the U.S. since 2005, totaling about $50 billion. This is 13 percent of China's global total. In 2012 alone, the U.S. was second to Canada in attracting investors, drawing a record $14.7 billion on the Heritage tally. This was nonetheless only the equivalent of less than 0.1 percent of 2012 GDP. Looking forward, Chinese investment in the U.S. could outpace investment growth globally, but there will undoubtedly be fits and starts. Cumulative investment should reach $100 billion within five years, still a relatively small amount.

The leading sector for investment in the U.S. has been finance, at a bit over $20 billion. This constitutes over half of Chinese non-bond investment in finance worldwide. Multiple large acquisitions occurred before the financial crisis and therefore lost considerable value. More active recently is energy and power, at $11.4 billion. This is just 6 percent of Chinese energy investment worldwide, indicating the American market has considerable potential in this regard.

Surprisingly, transport is the third-largest recipient in the U.S. at close to $6.5 billion, which constitutes almost 40 percent of China's global investment in transport (construction contracts are the more popular form of overseas transport business). But this is driven by a single transaction: the acquisition of AIG's aircraft leasing unit in December 2012.

Real estate and agriculture qualify as promising. Due partly to political and economic conditions in the PRC, there has been a surge in real estate purchases in the U.S. during the past two years and more are coming. Most are small-scale, but large-scale spending has also begun to appear. Agriculture is a missed opportunity: U.S. farmland should be more highly prized. In technology, despite the restrictions, the PRC's $2.5 billion investment in the U.S. is almost 30 percent of its global total. (The total does not include technology equipment contracts, where the U.S. is not involved.) Finally, the U.S. accounts for only 1 percent of Chinese metals investment.

With the leading role played by finance, the state of New York has drawn over two-fifths of Chinese investment in the U.S. If New York were a separate country, as some allege, it would be the fifth-largest recipient of Chinese investment. Next is Texas at 12 percent; no other state stands out. Only 17 states have drawn a Chinese investment of $100 million or more to date. This will change—more states are actively seeking investment and they will be successful. The American political debate over China policy will shift as a result.

The leading Chinese investor also follows directly from the emphasis on finance. China Investment Corporation (CIC), the smaller of the two sovereign wealth funds, is the undisputed king. CIC was created in part to diversify Chinese investments in the U.S. away from bonds, and aside from Hong Kong, the U.S. is its most important market. By itself, CIC accounts for over two-fifths of Chinese investment in the U.S. It was far less active in 2012, though, and may be seeking to reduce the U.S. weight in its holdings.

The larger wealth fund, the State Administration for Foreign Exchange (SAFE), is the next-largest investor at a bit under 10 percent of non-bond investment. SAFE is also the principal vehicle for purchases of American bonds. It is extremely secretive, and it would not be at all surprising if SAFE vehicles held more in American assets than can be documented. A small group of companies is in the $2 billion–$3 billion total investment range through end-2012. Oil major Sinopec is perhaps most notable among these, since it also is involved in large construction contracts here. As yet, very few Chinese companies have made the U.S. their top investment destination. If the environment remains stable, this will change.

The Heritage Tracker identifies parent companies, not subsidiaries. In terms of the volume of investment in the U.S., state entities predominate. From 2005 to 2012, they accounted for 86 percent of total investment, private entities 14 percent. However, in 2012 alone, the private share was almost double that, possibly indicating a new trend.

## WHY AND WHY NOT

Outward investment by any firm seeks something relatively lacking at home: additional demand (new market), physical assets, technology, labor force qualities, or simple financial return. The value of these is judged against the risk imposed by the political and regulatory environment.

Energy and metals—physical assets—have drawn by far the most Chinese investment globally. Farmland is similar but has not yet been made widely available. Finance and real estate are the next largest in size and aimed primarily at simple financial return. In transport, Chinese firms are looking to exploit their expertise by finding demand beyond the home market. Acquisitions of technology have been largely stymied. Across sectors, Chinese firms have long sought particular skills in foreign labor forces and now may seek cheap labor as the home labor market tightens.

On paper, the U.S. has everything an investor could want. It is by far the world's largest market. The U.S. has abundant land and energy assets, coal as well as shale. It is the world leader in technology and, arguably, skilled labor. The American real estate market has been more lucrative than China's for the past three years (Chinese investment in the U.S. has only an eight-year history). And American demand for transportation infrastructure is potentially quite high. The U.S. government does not need to do anything to make the country more attractive; the fundamentals are more than enough.

However, Chinese firms have not yet sought on a large scale to serve the American market through investment here. The U.S. does not permit most Chinese technology investment, with the medical sector an exception. This also reduces the scope for utilizing skilled labor. Energy assets were initially blocked, then perceived as blocked, and even now there is uncertainty over the acceptability of majority ownership in shale and any investment in coal. Banking drew heavy investment before the crisis; now real estate is drawing heavy investment. In practice, the main drivers of Chinese investment in the U.S. have been limited to perceived financial returns in banking and then real estate, supplemented by rising interest in American shale extraction.

One way to quantify the gap between the potential of the U.S. market for Chinese investment and its realization is Heritage's data on troubled transactions. The Heritage tally for the value of troubled Chinese investments in the U.S. between 2005 and 2012 is 15 transactions for about $30 billion, the most famous being CNOOC's attempted $18 billion acquisition of Unocal. (A $5 billion equipment contract was also blocked.) Had all of these been successful, total Chinese non-bond investment in the U.S. would have already reached at least $80 billion and probably more, since the Unocal failure was followed by an almost two-year lull in spending.

There are multiple reasons for the partial or complete transaction failures: (1) the inexperience of many Chinese firms; (2) American barriers; and (3) the role of the Chinese state. The first will fade over time. As more PRC firms become more knowledgeable about the U.S. market, they will be able to cater more to American consumers. Other PRC companies will learn which opportunities in land and transport are genuine. Parts of the American labor force will become more appealing. Sustained Chinese investment in the U.S. began only in 2007 and was carried by financials until 2010; there is still a great deal of space for learning. The second explanation for the unrealized market potential is U.S. government policy. In addition to CNOOC-Unocal, there are six cases of U.S. government actions that hampered or prohibited over $4 billion in investments. There are also potential projects that, in light of these failures, never moved forward. The latter point is critical both from a simple reading of the data and the clear consensus of Chinese executives: By far the most important U.S. government action to discourage investment is policy uncertainty.

For example, how exactly should other investors read the treatment of Huawei? American policymakers might think telecom has been clearly differentiated from any other sector, but the Chinese side does not. And there are matters that no American policymaker can possibly believe are transparent. Where does CFIUS's role end and Congress's begin? More narrowly, why did the $440 million acquisition of Nexteer's auto parts business sail through in 2010 but a $170 million minority investment in Steel Development's low-technology rebar production see sharp criticism a year later?

In general, what is available for investment and what is not? This is the most basic question for any investor, and the U.S. has failed to answer clearly with respect to many Chinese enterprises.

## STRATEGIC BEHAVIOR BY CHINESE ENTITIES

The third factor influencing Chinese investment choices in the U.S. is the Chinese state. There is almost surely a plan behind Chinese investment, both globally and in the U.S. State-owned enterprises dominate outward investment volume, making it feasible to have a coordinated strategy beyond simply seeking demand or higher financial return. More specifically, Beijing has repeatedly indicated that ownership of overseas commodities is a valuable means of ensuring the continuous imports the PRC's economy so badly needs. It is therefore no surprise that commodities investment by state firms dominates spending.

For the U.S., investment from 2007 to 2009 was almost entirely by a very small number of state financials. This certainly looks coordinated. The interest of the state oil majors in U.S. shale matches perfectly the interest of their government in diversifying energy sources and finding techniques to extract shale at home. More broadly, China's national interest in and corporate attempts to acquire technology to move up the value chain in production are no secret.

This is an important aspect of China's global investment strategy: it is not mysterious. Beijing perceives economic needs and strongly encourages state enterprises to meet them. The desire for resources and technology is well-known, as is the desire for national champions who can expand overseas. The foundations for Chinese outward investment are neither subtle nor, except for advanced dual-use technology, dangerous. They are also not especially sound. Metals investment feeds industries the central government constantly cites as suffering from sustained overcapacity. The PRC can catch up by buying foreign technology; by definition, it can never lead.

More specific sets of policies are equally unimpressive. The 12th Five-Year Plan discovered new strategic industries, adding them to the pile of old industries that should be fading but are still treated as strategic due to lack of political will. As a matter of economic development, the central government has shown little aptitude for identifying sectors to support, much less to abandon. In terms of outward investment, the loose guidance means most Chinese investments can be labeled strategic in policy terms, and the label thus has almost no real significance.

The challenge for the U.S. is not that Chinese industrial policies are especially effective; it is merely that the policies exist. Designated and aspiring national champions are handed the internal market and further subsidized in order to win global market share. They cannot go bankrupt and so no competition with them can be entirely fair. How to respond to the basic fact of state subsidization is a vital, well-established issue for the U.S. in dealing with the PRC; the additional matter of a grand investment strategy employing the subsidies is far from vital.

A second genuinely important issue concerns a second absence of transparency, this time on the Chinese side. SAFE in particular is a remarkably opaque organization and very likely has substantial indirect investments it is attempting to keep hidden.

The slim evidence of indirect acquisitions—an opaque Australia-based investor buying Japanese equities, a conspicuously timed surge in Cayman Islands purchases of U.S. Treasuries—indicates SAFE is probably interested in diversification and secrecy rather than dual-use technology. Indirect transactions by SAFE and others in the U.S. have focused on real estate and, to a lesser extent, autos. But SAFE's secretiveness plus several unwise choices by Chinese companies mean there are transactions whose nature was or is intended to be opaque, fueling suspicion.

The U.S. government can partly address this problem. Specific disclosure requirements can be formulated for financing vehicles, whether domiciled in the U.S. or elsewhere, receiving large sums from government arms or state firms. An example is SAFE's $2.5 billion contribution to one of TPG's funds in 2008. Stringent requirements, of course, will tend to reduce the capital inflow from SAFE and perhaps other entities. It would be better to have information voluntarily provided by the Chinese side and to take regulatory action only if such reasonable cooperation is not forthcoming.

Beyond additional disclosure, the Committee on Foreign Investment in the United States (CFIUS) must have clear authority to monitor indirect investments by any foreign entity, through foreign or domestic financial vehicles. A slow, unclear process will reduce investment, so the CFIUS mandate must also include strict operational guidelines. An intrusive CFIUS would be an unintended protectionist barrier, and also risk undermining the American goal of greater investment access to foreign markets.[2]

## CONCLUSION: TWEAK RATHER THAN TWIST

The U.S. does not desperately need policy steps to lure Chinese investment and avoid missing out on hundreds of billions of dollars in spending this decade. Nor does it need to embrace mercantilism to halt insidious Chinese technology acquisition for which there is precious little evidence. Chinese entities should be more transparent, preferably of their own accord but, if required, through regulation and quick, well-defined CFIUS action. This will ensure protection of sensitive technology, and the attractiveness of the American market will do the rest.

# Appendix 1

CHART 1

**Chinese Outward Investment Since 2005: Two Views**

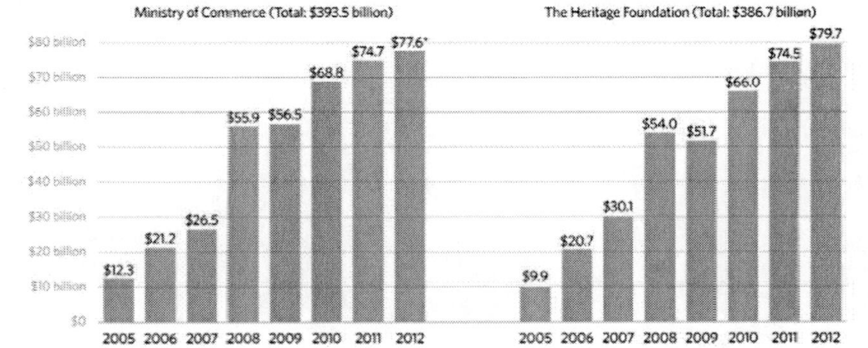


* Estimate based on extrapolating official figures for January through November.

**Sources:** The Heritage Foundation, China Global Investment Tracker dataset, updated January 2013, https://thf_media.s3.amazonaws.com/2013/xls/China-Global-Investment-Tracker2013.xls; Ministry of Commerce of the People's Republic of China, National Bureau of Statistics of the People's Republic of China, State Administration of Foreign Exchange, *2011 Statistical Bulletin of China's Outward Foreign Direct Investment*, China Statistics Press, August 2012; and Xinhua, "China's non-financial ODI grows at slower pace," December 18, 2012, http://english.peopledaily.com.cn/90778/8061743.html (accessed January 2, 2013).

B 2757 heritage.org

# Appendix 2

TABLE 1

## Sector Breakdown, 2005–2012

CHINESE BUSINESS ACTIVITY, IN BILLIONS OF DOLLARS

| Sector | Investment | Engineering contracts | Troubled |
|---|---|---|---|
| Energy and power | $186.1 | $97.2 | $75.4 |
| Metals | 90.2 | 8.6 | 57.7 |
| Finance | 37.3 | — | 29.2 |
| Real estate and construction | 21.7 | 27.6 | 7.2 |
| Transport | 16.6 | 72.9 | 15.0 |
| Agriculture | 11.8 | 6.8 | 9.5 |
| Technology | 8.7 | 4.9 | 13.3 |
| Chemicals | 6.2 | 2.1 | 0 |
| Other | 8.2 | 0 | 0.3 |
| **Total** | **$386.7** | **$219.9** | **$207.5** |

**Source:** The Heritage Foundation, China Global Investment Tracker dataset, updated January 2013, https://thf_media.s3.amazonaws.com/2013/xls/China-Global-Investment-Tracker2013.xls.

B 2757 heritage.org

# APPENDIX 3

MAP 1

**China's Worldwide Reach**

*North America drew the most Chinese investment in 2012 while sub-Saharan Africa had heavy engineering and construction activity by PRC firms.*

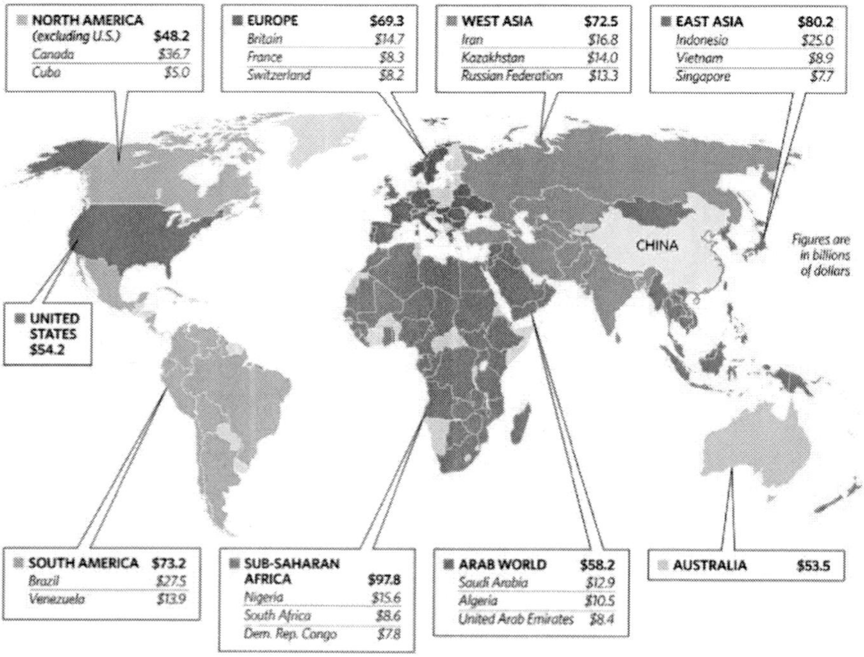


**Source:** The Heritage Foundation, China Global Investment Tracker dataset, updated January 2013, https://thf_media.s3.amazonaws.com/2013/xls/China-Global-Investment-Tracker2013.xls.

B 2757 heritage.org

## End Notes

[1] For a global overview, see Derek Scissors, "China's Global Investment Rises: The U.S. Should Focus on Competition," Heritage Foundation Backgrounder No. 2757, January 9, 2013, http://www.heritage.org/research/reports/2013/01/chinas-global-investment-rises-the-us-should-focus-oncompetition. For an interactive tool, see "China Global Investment Tracker Interactive Map," http://www.heritage.org/research/projects/china-global-investment-tracker-interactive-map.

[2] The proper role for CFIUS is an important issue deserving of separate discussion. See, for example, Derek Scissors, "A Better Committee on Foreign Investment in the United States," Heritage Foundation Issue Brief No. 3844, January 28, 2013, http://www.heritage.org/research/reports/2013/01/enhancing-the-committee-on-foreigninvestment-in-the-united-states-cfius.

In: China Investment Corporation
Editor: Ines Hembrecht
ISBN: 978-1-62808-913-4


*Chapter 4*

# TESTIMONY OF ANDREW SZAMOSSZEGI, PRINCIPAL, CAPITAL TRADE, INC. HEARING ON "TRENDS AND IMPLICATIONS OF CHINESE INVESTMENT IN THE UNITED STATES"*

Good morning. I'd like to thank to the Commission for having me here today to discuss the rationale for China's investment in the United States. It is an honor to appear not only before you, but also on a panel with Derek and Thilo.

My focus this morning is on the motives underlying Chinese investments in the United States and on the role played by the Chinese and U.S. governments.

## THE ROLE OF THE CHINESE GOVERNMENT

Chinese investments in the United States are motivated by both market forces and government policies and guidance. Despite China's indisputable liberalization in the areas of trade and investment during the past 34 years, Chinese enterprises continue to take their cues from government. The Chinese

* This is an edited, reformatted and augmented version of a testimony, presented May 9, 2013 before the U.S.-China Economic and Security Review Commission.

government has by varying degrees controlled the pace, direction, and composition of China's outward direct investment ("ODI").

This is largely a legacy of China's hard core communist past. Although Chinese multinational enterprises existed prior to 1949, China's ODI took a thirty-year hiatus following the formation of the Peoples Republic. Since then, the government has gone from the cautious liberalization of the late 1970s and early 1980s to limited promotion of the 1990s to the official embrace of ODI with the "Go Out" policy enunciated in 2001.

China's past avoidance of ODI placed the government in the role of gatekeeper once Beijing decided to allow outward investments, and it did not open the door and walk away.

As a gatekeeper, the Chinese government has had a pronounced impact on where China invests and in what sectors. When China first announced its "Go Out" policy, it was a major exporter with growing shares in advanced country markets, such as the United States. But rather than focus on those markets, China initially directed the bulk of its investments toward resource-rich countries, many of which were in Africa or members of OPEC. Indeed, Jiang Zemin's announcement of the "Go Out" policy identified Africa, Central Asia, the Middle East, Eastern Europe, and South America as favored destinations for Chinese investments.

The proclivity for resource-oriented investments is also evident in China's preference for investing in resource-rich advanced economies. According to OECD partner data, more than three quarters of China's FDI stocks in OECD countries were located in Australia and Canada, as opposed to the larger economies in Europe or the United States.

In general, there is a sense in China's government that ODI should also serve national aims, not just corporate ones. The Chinese government influences investments through a variety of policy documents, including the Overseas Investment Industrial Guidance Policy, which sets forth the broad parameters for investors; the Overseas Investment Industrial Guidance Catalogue, which provides specific details on the sectors where investments are encouraged; and the Five-Year Plans, which provide overall guidance on favored sectors.

For example, China's latest five-year plan calls for developing strategic emerging sectors, such as electric cars and biology-based industries, and clean energy technologies, such as the development and utilization of coal-bed gas and shale gas. These sectors feature prominently in China's U.S. investments.

## MAIN DRIVERS OF CHINA'S INVESTMENTS IN THE UNITED STATES

So, why are Chinese enterprises investing in the United States now? I'd like to start with the big picture: they have no choice. The United States has been a large net importer of goods and services over the past 35 years, and for the past 13 years, our largest deficits have been with China. This means that the United States must import capital and that China has trillions of dollars that it must recycle into U.S. assets. The Chinese government traditionally invested these dollars in U.S. government debt but several years ago decided to diversify its asset base into other U.S. investments. It created two large sovereign wealth funds to take make portfolio investments but these funds are passive investors, invest globally, and in any case cannot reasonably be expected to invest all of China's excess dollars. The only other alternative was to allow Chinese enterprises to significantly increase ODI to the U.S. market.

Sticking with the big picture, Chinese enterprises invest in the U.S. market because they can. Firms must have sufficient financial resources to invest abroad, especially when the host country is an advanced economy where asset prices are high. Twenty years ago, profits at Chinese firms were much smaller and the Yuan was weaker. Under those conditions, the number of Chinese firms that could have invested in the United States was fairly limited. Today, the Yuan is stronger relative to the dollar, the absolute level of profits in China is much higher, and Chinese investors are more sophisticated. They also have access to top M&A legal talent in Hong Kong. Thus Chinese enterprises today are much more capable of investing in the United States than was the case even a decade ago.

My final "big picture" reason for Chinese investments in the United States is that the financial crisis and subsequent recession created many bargains for Chinese investors. For example, Morgan Stanley was selling at a 40 percent discount when one of China's sovereign wealth funds obtained a nearly 10-percent stake in December 2007. CIC and other private investors have also made many investments in U.S. real estate, either directly through property purchases or indirectly through property funds. But bargain hunting also took place in the manufacturing sector in industries such as solar, auto parts, and advanced batteries.

Aside from the big picture explanations, there are a number of industry and firm-specific reasons why certain Chinese firms are investing in particular U.S. industries. These include:

- maintaining or increasing U.S. market share in the face of trade remedies, such as antidumping and countervailing duties;
- acquiring technology and other strategic assets (such as distribution networks and brands);
- participating in U.S. sectors deemed important to the Chinese government; and
- making money.

Chinese firms from certain industries have invested in order to insulate their U.S. exports from trade remedies. Chinese producers are currently subject to 121 antidumping and countervailing duty orders. Chinese firms in some industries have sought to avoid the consequences of trade remedies by shipping to the United States illegally through third markets or by establishing export platforms outside of China. Other Chinese firms from the steel, aluminum, and solar panel industries have attempted to invest in the United States to avoid existing trade remedy orders or preempt an investigation.

Firms in industries favored by Chinese government policies have also sought to expand in the U.S. market through FDI. Two recent examples are Anshan, a major state-owned steel producer, and Suntech, a private manufacturer of solar panels. Anshan's efforts were unsuccessful and it never invested, while Suntech established a facility in Arizona.

It is worth dwelling on Suntech's investment because it provides a vivid illustration of how the intersection of Chinese government policies and market forces can lead to foreign investments and market distortions that are harmful to U.S. industries.

China's five-year plans have been promoting the expansion of renewable energy industries in China since the mid-1990s. The 11$^{th}$ Five-Year Plan and other contemporaneous measures explicitly encouraged production of renewable energy and continued industry incentives. The government funded national R&D efforts aimed at solar and other renewable technologies and provided financial incentives. As described by Keith Bradsher in one of his excellent New York Times articles on China's solar industry, "Chinese governments at the national, provincial and even local level have been competing with one another to offer solar companies ever more generous subsidies, including free land, and cash for research and development. State-owned banks are flooding the industry with loans at considerably lower interest rates than available in Europe or the United States."

Even more important than government funding in my view is the signal that such official imprimatur sent to private investors. Major Chinese producers were able to leverage government support into hundreds of millions of dollars' worth of private capital. This in turn fueled a reckless expansion in China that caused solar panel prices to drop precipitously worldwide, leading to plant shutdowns and insolvencies in the United States, Europe, and even China.

Though Suntech closed its Arizona facility, local governments in China and China's policy banks have been keeping the major producers in China afloat with subsidized access to capital, prolonging depressed prices in the United States and Europe.

The recent experience with the Chinese solar industry is very instructive and something that we should be mindful of going forward. As distortive as China's subsidies and targeting have been in the past, the solar industry has shown what can happen when you throw vast sums of private capital into the mix. The effects can be dramatic and have devastating consequences to firms in emerging industries that are being targeted by Beijing in China's 12th Five-year Plan.

Another reason why Chinese firms invest in the United States is because the amount of red tape is less of a problem in the United States than it is in China. Unless there are national security concerns, or investments in sensitive U.S. sectors by state-owned enterprises or their subsidiaries, investing in the United States is not very difficult. Also, if you are a privately owned firm, you probably have a more level playing field for accessing capital in the United States than you do in China, where state-owned banks continue to give favorable treatment to state-owned firms.

Gaining access to U.S. capital markets seems to be the primary motive of enterprises that have purchased listed U.S. shell companies through reverse mergers. From 2007 to 2011, more Chinese firms entered U.S. capital markets through reverse mergers than through IPOs by a ratio of three to one. In the typical reverse merger, a Chinese enterprise purchases a listed firm that has few if any assets. This technique is typically used by private firms that have difficulty accessing capital in China or by provincial SOEs trying to support restructuring efforts in China.

There have been a series of de-listings and huge drops in the share prices of more than two dozen Chinese firms that initially listed in the United States via reverse mergers. As a result of numerous instances of poor financial reporting and outright fraud involving Chinese reverse mergers, the SEC approved new rules in November 2011 and the Public Company Accounting Oversight Board has tried to negotiate with China's Ministry of Finance (MOF) to allow more oversight of Chinese accounting firms. Many investors have been burned, but there is also research showing that Chinese reverse mergers have performed better than reverse mergers in which the purchasing entity was a U.S. firm.

The point I want to make is that although the initial purchase of U.S. assets by Chinese firms may seem like Chinese FDI in the United States, the flow of money is more likely to be from the United States to China.

Aside from making money, the main motivations for investing in the United States are technology acquisition and market access. Technology acquisition is a major goal of Chinese government policies. These days the focus is on cyber espionage, but Chinese policies toward inward and outward FDI are also geared to promote the flow of technology from advanced countries to China. Technology related investments frequently involve firms with state ties; some notable examples include government-owned Anshan Iron and Steel and Huawei, which has long been suspected of having ties to the Chinese military. Chinese firms have also made a number of investments in which the goal was obtaining energy-related technology, advanced battery technology in particular. Examples include:

- Yingtong Energy's Altair Nanotechnologies, a producer of lithium titanate batteries;
- Wanxiang's purchase of A123, a U.S. producer of lithium ion batteries for automotive and utility applications;
- A private equity purchase of lithium battery maker Boston Power, a deal that triggered financial incentives provided by the Chinese government;
- Sinopec's purchase of Syntroleum, which operated a gas-to-liquid demonstration facility and supplied military bases with fuels;
- Sinopec's purchase of a stake in certain Devon Energy shale gas fields; and
- CNOOC International Limited's purchase of an ownership stake in Chesapeake Energy's shale oil plays in Wyoming, Colorado, and Texas.

I think that the hand of the government is plainly visible in all these investments, with the possible exception of Wanxiang's investment in A123. In some cases, the investing companies stated unequivocally that the investment was made to acquire technology and know-how. In others, production was moved to China.

## U.S. GOVERNMENT POLICIES AND CHINESE INVESTORS

At first blush, U.S. policy toward Chinese investment seems schizophrenic. On the one hand, there is the Committee on Foreign Investments in the United States (CFIUS), which examines the national security aspects of potential investments and has had a hand in derailing investments by CNOOC (Unocal) and Huawei (3-Com and 3Leaf Systems). Various members of Congress have criticized specific Chinese investments and expressed their concerns about investments by Chinese state-owned enterprises quite forcefully.

On the other hand, SelectUSA of the Department of Commerce is courting Chinese investments and working with states to attract Chinese FDI. Other politicians are trumpeting their roles in bringing Chinese investments to their states.

Oddly enough, this hodgepodge makes perfect sense. The federal government is responsible for national security and has put in place a system to review transactions with potential security implications. China presents new challenges because investments by SOEs can blur the line between national and economic security. Congress has responded by strengthening CFIUS through the Foreign Investment and National Security Act of 2007.

State governments are more concerned with attracting investments to support jobs and economic growth and do not care much if the investor is a state-owned enterprise. For Congressmen with limited constituencies in manufacturing industries, attracting Chinese investments has little downside.

So, there is obviously a tension here, but it is a healthy one that can weed out potentially threatening investments.

The response of the Security and Exchange Commission and the Public Company Accounting Oversight Board to the problems caused by reverse mergers involving fraudulent accounting by Chinese firms is also noteworthy. Some may say that it is unfair to single out Chinese reverse mergers when all reverse mergers are risky. Here again, the policy response has been a healthy one; from what I have seen in my work, the concerns expressed about the credibility of audited financial statements are well founded. Washington has not prohibited reverse mergers, but instead taken steps to ensure that the Chinese companies which enter the U.S. capital markets via reverse mergers are legitimate.

Chinese investments in the United States are subject to the same set of rules and regulations as investments from other foreign countries in the areas of foreign corrupt practices, export administration, sanctions, and antitrust. If

Chinese firms run afoul of these rules, they should expect to pay the price, as ZTE has done due to its business with Iran. The one area where Chinese firms are subject to additional scrutiny is in the networking sector, where cyber-security and other concerns with Huawei and ZTE have led to greater scrutiny of those firms and legislation that requires federal agencies to get approval from cyber-espionage investigators before buying IT systems from Chinese companies.

## CLOSING THOUGHTS

Historically, foreign direct investments in the United States have emanated from advanced, market-oriented economies or oil exporters recycling petrol dollars, neither of which posed much of a national security threat. China is different and U.S. policies have had to adjust. By and large, these measured responses have created an environment that allows investments from China to continue, while reducing the potential for adverse security and economic outcomes.

In: China Investment Corporation
Editor: Ines Hembrecht

ISBN: 978-1-62808-913-4


*Chapter 5*

# TESTIMONY OF ELIZABETH DRAKE, PARTNER, LAW OFFICES OF STEWART AND STEWART. HEARING ON "TRENDS AND IMPLICATIONS OF CHINESE INVESTMENT IN THE UNITED STATES"*

## I. INTRODUCTION

China's global outbound foreign direct investment ("FDI") reached another record level in 2012, exceeding $77 billion.[2] The United States continues to be the top destination for China's outbound FDI, receiving at least $17 billion in Chinese investment in 2012 according to one estimate.[3] While still a relatively small portion of total inbound FDI in the United States, China's investment activities deserve attention from policymakers for a number of reasons.

As a preliminary matter, investment from China will become an increasingly important part of the country's inbound flows: by 2020, China's global outbound investment stock is poised to reach $2 trillion, more than six times what it was in 2010.[4] Policymakers should thus be approaching Chinese investment not merely on the basis of investments that have already been made, but also on the basis of what is likely to occur in the near future.

* This is an edited, reformatted and augmented version of a testimony, presented May 9, 2013 before the U.S.-China Economic and Security Review Commission.

Moreover, the Government of China has an explicit policy to encourage and support outbound FDI, and provides significant government support to such investment through state funding and financing from state-owned banks. Domestic firms and workers who enjoy no such support can thus be put at a severe competitive disadvantage if Chinese firms with such aggressive government backing become their closest competitors.

In addition, China's outbound FDI is unique in the extent to which it is dominated by state-invested and state-owned firms (collectively, "SOEs"). In 2012, for example, it is estimated that private firms accounted for only 9.5% of China's outbound FDI to the world.[5] These SOEs continue to be heavily influenced and supported by the state, and they may have a variety of non-commercial motives for their investments. These motivations may raise concerns not only about national security, but also about economic security.

While there are potential benefits as well as challenges posed by Chinese investment in the United States, this testimony focuses on three areas in which Chinese investment may undermine U.S. competitiveness and economic opportunities. The three areas are: 1) price competition with Chinese-invested firms in the U.S. market; 2) trade distortions that may result from Chinese investors' supply chain policies; and 3) competition for resources and technology.

This testimony recommends policies to address the challenges posed by increased Chinese investment in each of these three areas. While some of these recommendations could be implemented by adapting current policy instruments, the challenges posed by Chinese investment would be best addressed by a comprehensive U.S. policy response. To the extent that existing policy tools are inadequate, policymakers should consider creating new remedies to ensure that Chinese investment does not distort the competitive playing field for workers and firms in the United States.

## II. Price Competition with Chinese-Invested Firms

As noted above, the Chinese government has an explicit policy supporting overseas FDI, and it aggressively supports such investment with government funding and financing from state-owned banks. As part of its "going out" strategy, the Government of China has developed specific investment funds to promote outward investment in natural resources and in fields with technological promise.[6] In addition, China's Export-Import Bank and the China Development Bank have poured billions of dollars into supporting overseas investments, with credits that are reportedly available at highly concessional rates.[7] Furthermore, SOEs that benefit from direct Chinese government funding, and are subject to Chinese government policy direction, make up the vast majority of Chinese investment. These firms do not face the same market discipline or incentives as private firms. They can rely on state support to maintain losses that may never be recouped, and make other operating decisions on a non-commercial basis, in order to meet political or industrial policy goals.

The direct support and involvement of the Chinese government can give Chinese firms (and Chinese-invested firms) important advantages in the U.S. market that their competitors do not enjoy. When a U.S. firm has to obtain credit at market rates to finance its activities, but a Chinese firm can obtain financing at minimal or even zero percent interest from Chinese state-owned banks, it distorts competition in the United States market. Such state support permits a Chinese firm to make investments and acquire resources and technology it otherwise could not if it had to pay market rates for equity and finance. In addition, such state support may permit Chinese firms to make decisions regarding the sales prices of their goods and services that do not reflect market fundamentals and that undercut their U.S. competitors.

Current U.S. law does not adequately protect U.S. workers and firms from this type of unfair competition. Existing antitrust rules, for example, are based on assumptions about the profit-maximizing behavior of market actors that simply may not apply to certain Chinese firms. In the area of predatory pricing, the U.S. applies a recoupment test, under which pricing is only deemed anti-competitive if the predator is likely to eventually collect enough profits to make up for the losses caused by the predatory behavior.[8] The test is based on the theory that a predator who could not recoup its losses would either not engage in the predatory practices to begin with or will eventually exit the market, causing no long-term damage to competitors or consumers. A Chinese SOE, by contrast, may be able to rely on state support to maintain losses that may never be recouped, and engage in predatory pricing in order to gain U.S. market share in the furtherance of political or industrial policy goals. Such a firm could engage in predatory pricing behavior that causes severe damage to its U.S. competitors, but, under current law, such behavior would not be considered anticompetitive as long as the Chinese firm was not expected to recoup its losses.

In addition, existing anti-subsidy disciplines in U.S. countervailing duty law and at the World Trade Organization do not address the harm caused by competition with subsidized investors. U.S. countervailing duty law only addresses the injury caused by subsidized imports of goods, not investments by subsidized firms. WTO rules permit relief on the basis of harm in a range of markets, including third-country markets and the market of the subsidizing government itself, but these rules similarly focus on the harm that arises from competing with subsidized goods, not firms. Finally, though China committed to ensure that Chinese SOEs would make decisions on their purchases and sales on commercial terms when it joined the WTO, these commitments have never been tested. It is highly unlikely that the WTO would enforce such commitments regarding decisions that are made by SOEs operating outside of China.

## III. Trade Distortions Linked to Chinese Investment

Several analysts have noted that one motivation for Chinese investment is access to markets that are otherwise restricted by trade barriers.[9] Such barriers may include prevailing tariff rates as well as duties imposed to counteract unfair trade practices, such as antidumping and countervailing duties. While U.S. trade remedy laws allow an antidumping or countervailing duty order to be expanded to cover imported parts that are used to assemble merchandise in the U.S. that would otherwise be subject to unfair trade duties, relief is only available if the assembly in the U.S. is insignificant and if the value of imported components is a significant portion of total value.[10] The Department of Commerce also considers affiliation between the assembler in the U.S. and the component exporter, among other factors. These rules may be inadequate to redress the harm that U.S. workers and firms may suffer if a Chinese company invests in the U.S. to evade trade remedies, especially where the investor's operations in the U.S. are not insignificant or where the investor is not directly affiliated with the Chinese component producer.

In addition, Chinese SOEs in particular have been known to discriminate against non-Chinese producers in making sourcing decisions. The state-owned wind turbine producer Sinovel, for example, required its American component supplier to agree to a "localization schedule" under which components which it had produced with non-Chinese material would instead be produced with

Chinese materials.[11] More recently, as part of an agreement to establish a joint-venture with a Chinese SOE to produce trucks, Daimler similarly agreed to "localize" the production of the truck engines to China.[12] While these agreements pertained to supply agreements and investments in China, the same motivations to fulfill Chinese industrial policies may lead Chinese investors to discriminate against non-Chinese goods when producing in the United States. Increased investment by such firms in the United States could result in increased imports from China, placing U.S. suppliers at a disadvantage.

There are currently no remedies available for workers or producers who may be harmed by such discrimination. WTO rules that prohibit discrimination against non-Chinese goods by the Government of China, for example, apply to its treatment of those goods upon importation into China – they would not apply to discrimination that takes place against foreign goods that are not imported into China. In addition, as noted above, while China committed to ensure that Chinese SOEs would make decisions on their purchases and sales on commercial terms when it joined the WTO, these commitments have never been tested, and it is highly unlikely that the WTO would enforce such commitments regarding decisions that are made by SOEs operating outside of China.

## IV. COMPETITION FOR RESOURCES AND TECHNOLOGY

Part of the motivation for China's promotion of outward FDI is to gain access to valuable resources and technology.[13] As noted above, the Government of China has established two funds to support outbound investment dedicated specifically for these purposes. Chinese firms that use such government support may be able to outbid U.S. producers for critical resources and technology, negatively impacting U.S. competitiveness. In addition, Chinese firms may not only outbid their U.S. competitors but be able to monopolize access to the technology, harming the U.S. economy as a whole. While private firms operating on a commercial basis also make investment decisions in order to access resources and technology, in some cases decisions by Chinese firms in this regard (especially by SOEs) may be influenced by non-commercial factors such as government policy priorities.

For example, in 1995, a group of companies that included Chinese SOEs sought to acquire Magnaquench, the only U.S. producer of neodymium-iron-boron magnets.[14] The magnets are an important technology for MRIs, wind turbines, automotive motors, and a wide array of other applications. The magnets also have critical military applications, including target lasers, satellite communications systems, radar amplifiers, and more.[15] The investment was approved on the basis of a commitment from the investors to keep production of the magnets in the United States for at least five years.[16] The day after the five-year period expired, the investors closed the facility, laid off the workers, and took the equipment and technology to China.[17] By 2007, China had more than 130 enterprises engaged in manufacturing the critical permanent magnets; the U.S. had none.[18]

Current U.S. policies are insufficient to ensure that U.S. producers will be able to compete on a level playing field to acquire and maintain access to key resources and technologies. The Committee on Foreign Investment in the United States ("CFIUS") process, for example, is designed to screen foreign investment for national security concerns, but not economic security or competitiveness issues. Thus, while CFIUS applies heightened scrutiny to transactions involving SOEs that may impact national security, it does not screen investments for their economic impacts. In addition, while the Department of Justice reviews proposed mergers and acquisitions for potential competitiveness concerns, these typically relate to market dominance in general rather than specific concerns about strategic resources or technologies. Other countries do screen foreign investment for such issues. Australia and Canada, for example, apply a net benefit test when evaluating proposed foreign investment, and the test includes economic, as well as national security, criteria.

## V. Options for Policymakers

There are a number of options policymakers should consider to maximize the benefits, and minimize the potential threat, of Chinese investment in the United States. The U.S. should take a comprehensive approach to ensure, among other things, that:

1) U.S. workers and firms will not be undercut by unfair competition from firms operating in the U.S. that benefit from foreign government support or operate under the control of foreign government entities, including (but not limited to) the Government of China;

2) foreign investment does not undermine the effectiveness of our trade remedy laws nor entail discrimination against United States suppliers of goods and services; and
3) U.S. producers enjoy access to key resources and technologies on commercial terms and are not deprived of such access due to unfair competition with foreign investors.

U.S. policy should also draw on the principle of competitive neutrality, especially with regard to competition with China's SOEs. The *OECD Guidelines on Corporate Governance of State-Owned Enterprises* offer guidance in this area. For example, Chapter I of the *Guidelines* states that governments should ensure a "level playing field" in markets where SOEs and private companies compete "in order to avoid market distortions."[19] Thus, "SOEs should face competitive conditions regarding access to finance," and SOEs' relationships with state-owned banks and other SOEs "should be based on purely commercial grounds."[20] The *OECD Guidelines* also state that SOEs should disclose material information on all matters described in the *Guidelines*, including "[a]ny financial assistance, including guarantees, received from the state and commitments made on behalf of the SOE," material transactions with related entities, and material risk factors.[21]

One way to meet these goals would be to get China to agree to binding obligations regarding its outbound FDI based on the principles of competitive neutrality. While the U.S. already secured some obligations from China regarding the operations of its SOEs in China's accession to the WTO, these obligations apply to those firms' operations within China – not to their investments abroad. New disciplines should, at a minimum, require transparency and disclosure as to the extent of state support, ownership, and control. All firms should be required to operate on the basis of competitive neutrality, with business decisions made on the basis of commercial considerations rather than government policies (whether those decision relate to pricing, sourcing, or acquisition of resources and technology). To be meaningful, such obligations would need to be enforceable through a dispute settlement mechanism and the prospect of economic consequences for non-compliance.

In addition, the U.S. should take proactive steps to seek enforcement of those obligations China has undertaken to date. At the WTO, for example, the U.S. should challenge prohibited subsidies such as export credits on terms that do not comply with the terms of the OECD arrangement, as well as SOEs' use of domestic content and technology transfer requirements in their procurement and investment contracts. If these rules prove to be effective, they may provide an appropriate template for future disciplines on the actions of SOEs outside of their home country boundaries. If not, those disciplines need to be not only expanded in scope but also strengthened in substance. In the context of the on-going Trans-Pacific Partnership negotiations, for example, parties are reportedly discussing the inclusion of rules that would discipline the actions of SOEs and seek to ensure that they behave on commercial terms. Such disciplines should also be included in the model Bilateral Investment Treaty the U.S. relies upon in negotiating investment agreements with other countries. These rules must set a high standard that addresses not only potential concerns with TPP or BIT partners, but also with other major trading and investing countries we may negotiate with in the future, such as China.

Whether or not the U.S. is able to secure binding commitments from China regarding its outbound FDI, the U.S. can take unilateral action to minimize the negative impacts such investment may have on the U.S. economy. Policymakers should first consider improving the process for screening new investments in the U.S., particularly investments by firms that are supported or controlled by foreign governments. Such investments should be reviewed from the standpoint of competitive neutrality, and be reviewed for their economic, as well as national security, implications. As a condition of investment approval, the U.S. should require such investors to disclose material information such as levels of government support and the basis for pricing and procurement practices. The U.S. should require that such firms operate in a manner that is consistent with competitive neutrality principles, meaning that prices, sourcing decisions, and other business decisions are made on a commercial basis and free from foreign government influence. To meet these commitments, the U.S. may also require that directors and officers of the U.S. entity be independent from the foreign government, consistent with Australia's practice in some cases.[22] The U.S. should require regular reporting and monitoring to ensure these commitments are met. In addition, when the Department of Justice reviews proposed mergers and acquisitions for competition concerns, it should take into account whether the investor benefits from foreign government support and whether the investor is owned or controlled by a foreign government entity and thus may operate in a manner that is not consistent with commercial considerations.

There must also be a means for U.S. workers and firms to seek redress where they have suffered competitive harm, or are threatened with harm, due to unfair competition with foreign investors. While certain tools already exist in domestic competition laws, these tools should be re-evaluated to ensure that they adequately address competition with firms that benefit from foreign government support or are controlled by foreign governments. Predatory pricing rules, for example, may need to be revised to permit alternative means of establishing predatory behavior where the firms involved are subsidized by the government or there are other indications that they do not operate on a commercial basis. Instead of applying the recoupment test to determine if prices are predatory, for example, cost benchmarks could be used to evaluate the prices charged. Evidence of foreign government influence on, or support for, pricing decisions may also be relevant to such inquiries. Competition laws should also be reviewed to determine whether discrimination against domestic origin goods on the basis of a purchasing firm's foreign government support or control rather than commercial considerations should be considered an anticompetitive practice.

Ultimately, the law should give a private right of action to U.S. firms and workers that have been harmed by subsidized and SOE investment in the United States. Such a right of action should cover harm due to anticompetitive behavior as well as harm stemming from discriminatory and non-commercial purchasing decisions. If harm is shown, the injured party should be entitled to compensation for lost revenues, lost wages, and other damages. Allegations of such behavior should also trigger an investigation by the screening mechanism proposed above to determine whether any of the conditions of investment approval have been breached.

In addition, domestic trade remedy laws may need to be strengthened to ensure they cannot be circumvented through foreign investment, particularly state-backed foreign investment. As noted above, current rules on circumvention of antidumping and countervailing duty orders through investments in domestic production depend, in part, on whether the domestic investment is insignificant and on the affiliation between the investor and the foreign component producer or exporter. To the extent such limitations pose an obstacle to effective enforcement of the unfair trade laws, they should be altered or eliminated.

Finally, policymakers should ensure that the other policy tools we already do have available are being used to the furthest extent possible to minimize the risks that foreign government-backed investment from China (and other countries) may pose. The CFIUS process, for example, should exercise its mandate to protect national security concerns in the broadest sense of the term, and learn from the practices of other countries regarding the undertakings that state-owned investors are required to agree to when investments implicate national security concerns. Buy America rules may need to be examined to determine whether the fact that a bidder is an SOE or a subsidized firm should be taken into account when determining contract awards. Finally, the SEC should clarify that state support for, and control over, an enterprise are material items that require disclosure in the interest of protecting private investors. The terms of state assistance and financing to SOEs, the terms of supply and procurement contracts with state-owned suppliers and purchasers, and the relationship between a firm's directors and officers and the government should all be considered material information for which disclosure is required.

## End Notes

[1] This testimony reflects the individual views of the author, and not necessarily the views of the Law Offices of Stewart and Stewart or any of its clients.

[2] "The expanding scale and scope of China's outward direct investment," The Economist (Jan. 19, 2013).

[3] Heritage Foundation, "China Global Investment Tracker," available on-line at: http://www.heritage.org/research/projects/china-global-investment-tracker-interactive-map.

[4] Shuping Liao and Yongsheng Zhang, "Strategies for Managing China's State-Owned Foreign Direct Investment," EABER Working Paper Series Paper No. 76 (Aug. 20, 2012) at 6-7.

[5] "The expanding scale and scope of China's outward direct investment," The Economist (Jan. 19, 2013).

[6] Huang Webin and Andreas Wilkes, "Analysis of China's overseas investment policies," CIFOR Working Paper 79 (2011) at 12-13.

[7] Id. See also Terence P. Stewart, et al., China's Support Programs for Automobiles and Auto Parts under the 12th Five-Year Plan (Jan. 2012) at 60.

[8] Antonio Capobianco and Hans Christiansen, "Competitive Neutrality and State-Owned Enterprises: Challenges and Policy Options," OECD Corporate Governance Working Papers No. 1 (2011) at 21.

[9] Nargiza Salidjanova, "Going Out: An Overview of China's Outward Foreign Direct Investment," U.S.-China Economic & Security Review Commission Staff Research Report (Mar. 30, 2011) at 10-11.

[10] 19 U.S.C. Sec. 1677j(a).

[11] American Superconductor Corp. Form 8-K (June 5, 2008) at Ex. 10.1. See also American Superconductor Corp. Form 10-Q (Aug. 5, 2010) at 18.

[12] "Germany's Daimler to Make Trucks in China," Agence France Presse (Spet. 26, 2011); "Final Approval Issued by Chinese Authorities: Way Clear for Daimler's Truck Joint Venture with Foton," Daimler.com (Sept. 26, 2011).

[13] Huang Webin and Andreas Wilkes, "Analysis of China's overseas investment policies," CIFOR Working Paper 79 (2011) at 9. See also Nargiza Salidjanova, "Going Out: An Overview of China's Outward Foreign Direct Investment," U.S.-China Economic & Security Review Commission Staff Research Report (Mar. 30, 2011) at 7-9.

[14] Cindy Hurst, "China's Rare Earth Elements Industry: What Can the West Learn?" Institute for the Analysis of Global Security (March 2010) at 12. See also Karl P. Sauvant, "Investing in

the United States: Is the US Ready for FDI from China?" Edward Elgar Studies in International Investment (2009) at 46.

[15] Cindy Hurst, "China's Rare Earth Elements Industry: What Can the West Learn?" Institute for the Analysis of Global Security (March 2010) at 13.

[16] Id.

[17] Id.

[18] Id.

[19] OECD Guidelines on Corporate Governance of State-Owned Enterprises, Ch. I, chapeau.

[20] Id. at Ch. I, Sec. F.

[21] Id. at Ch. V, Sec. E.

[22] Greg Golding, "Australian regulation of foreign direct investment by sovereign wealth funds and State-owned enterprises: Are our rules right?" (2010) 38 ABLR 215, 227.

In: China Investment Corporation
Editor: Ines Hembrecht
ISBN: 978-1-62808-913-4


*Chapter 6*

# TESTIMONY OF MARK E. PLOTKIN[1], PARTNER, COVINGTON & BURLING LLP. HEARING ON "TRENDS AND IMPLICATIONS OF CHINESE INVESTMENT IN THE UNITED STATES"*

Thank you to the Commission and, in particular, to Commissioners Bartholomew and Wortzel for convening this hearing and offering me the opportunity to participate. Chinese investment in the United States is an important policy issue for our nation, and I am honored to be asked to contribute to the Commission's work in this regard.

The subject of this particular panel is "Issues for Policymakers" and I accordingly will focus on the current state of U.S. law and policy concerning Chinese investment in the United States. My perspective is informed by my experience as an attorney representing parties involved in cross-border transactions, including before the Committee on Foreign Investment in the United States, or CFIUS. Many of these cases have involved Chinese investors. In some instances I represent sellers of U.S. assets, while in other instances I advise Chinese buyers of such assets. In these circumstances, I have developed some views as to how our laws and policies governing foreign investment in the United States are implemented and how they impact trade, commerce and U.S. national security.

* This is an edited, reformatted and augmented version of a testimony, Presented May 9, 2013 before the U.S.-China Economic and Security Review Commission.

I have three principal points to offer the Commission.

*First*, I believe that existing U.S. law is adequate to protect our national security interests. Although I may disagree at times with how the law is implemented, I submit that the dedicated individuals and institutions charged with protecting our national security have available to them the necessary legal tools to carry out their duties effectively and efficiently. In particular, CFIUS is a powerful institution because the Congress wisely crafted its statutory mandate with what I term "living" language — language that permits the Committee and its constituent agencies to adapt readily to a constantly evolving national security landscape. I urge the Commission to resist recommending any additional categorical requirements that would impede the Committee's ability to evaluate each transaction on a case-by-case basis in the context of the current security environment.

*Second*, CFIUS as structured pursuant to the Exon-Florio amendment was expressly designed to evaluate whether a proposed transaction threatens to impair U.S. national security. I believe that it would be an error to expand the Committee's mandate to include assessing the economic effects of a transaction, such as through a so-called "net benefit" test. A net benefit test would be inconsistent with our country's longstanding policy of open investment, it would be outside of CFIUS's institutional competence, and it would be inappropriate for a regulatory body that operates in secret. It also would risk detracting from the Committee's core function of protecting our national security and could unintentionally lend credence to allegations that CFIUS is a trade barrier dressed up as a national security tool.

*Third*, we should remember that foreign direct investment and national security need not be zero sum in combination. More Chinese investment does not mean that we are less secure. The goal of our laws and policies should be two-fold: to encourage foreign investment *and* to protect national security. I have seen for myself that the two need not be mutually exclusive. Rather, handled correctly, appropriately tailored CFIUS mitigation can permit Chinese and other foreign investment in the United States while actually enhancing U.S. national security at the very same time. In this respect, CFIUS — when utilized adroitly — can be an economic and a security tool of equal force using just the existing legal authorities available today. Our nation and our people will be best served when we can pursue both our security and economic goals in a manner that is complementary rather than exclusive.

Let me turn first to the adequacy of existing law to protect our interests.

# I. The Adequacy of Existing Law to Address Chinese Investment

## A. U.S. National Security Review of Foreign Investment

As I mentioned, I believe that CFIUS's strength comes from the "living" language of its statutory mandate, which leaves the phrase "national security" undefined and subject to the Committee's interpretation and discretion. This flexibility is crucial because national security is not a static concept. Our security interests change as we evolve as a nation and as the world shifts around us. If this hearing were held in 1988 when the Exon-Florio amendment was enacted, the topic of cyber security never would have arisen. Now cyber security is a critical part of nearly every CFIUS review. As this Commission is well aware, the past decade has seen heightened focus on China as a strategic competitor and economic partner. And CFIUS has responded by intensifying its scrutiny of proposed Chinese investments. At the same time, other issues have faded. The fears about Middle Eastern investment that drove the creation of CFIUS in the 1970s, and the concerns about Japanese investment that were the impetus for the Exon-Florio amendment in the 1980s, have largely dissipated. None of us can imagine, let alone predict, the primary issues that CFIUS will face 20 years hence.

CFIUS's statutory mandate is simultaneously narrow in scope and vague in its application. The Committee has the power to review certain transactions to "determine the effects of the transaction on the national security of the United States."[2] The statute was amended in 2008 by the Foreign Investment and National Security Act ("FINSA") to specify that national security shall be construed to include issues related to homeland security, but national security is not otherwise defined.[3] The statute provides a list of factors that the Committee must consider, but these factors are neither intended to be an exhaustive definition of the scope of national security nor are they treated as such in practice.[4] National security also is left undefined by the Department of the Treasury's regulations implementing FINSA.[5]

Because of this "living language," the CFIUS agencies are free to interpret national security consistent with their individual mandates and equities, instead of being locked into a rigid statutory box. Simply by way of example, the Department of Energy focuses on potential threats to our energy infrastructure, while the Department of Homeland Security concentrates on critical infrastructure, and the Department of Commerce scrutinizes compliance with export control regulations. Permitting the CFIUS member agencies to apply their own definitions of national security ensures that a broad range of interests are represented, weighed, and balanced as part of the review process.

Cyber security offers a topical and compelling example of how CFIUS has adapted to a changing national security landscape. Neither the Exon-Florio amendment nor FINSA make any mention of cyber security. Yet cyber issues play a significant role in nearly every review and investigation. The Commission may be considering whether to recommend a specific statutory requirement that CFIUS conduct a cyber security analysis for each transaction it reviews. I would caution against such a mandate for two reasons. First, it is unnecessary. As the threat of cyber attacks and cyber espionage has increased, I have seen CFIUS focus more acutely on cyber security in its reviews, investigations, and mitigation agreements, especially where there is a Chinese investor. The CFIUS regulations also specifically require the parties to submit details related to cyber security practices.[6]

Separately, unnecessary mandates have the potential to distract from other, more pressing national security risks presented by a transaction. I have never seen two transactions that were the same, or even largely similar. The nature and severity of the potential risks vary widely. In some cases, cyber security is the chief risk and should be the focus of the Committee's review. In other cases, it may be appropriate for the Committee to commit its resources elsewhere, such as assessing geographic proximity concerns (in CFIUS parlance, "persistent co-location") or regulatory compliance matters. A mandatory cyber security analysis would risk redirecting the Committee's limited resources from more pressing matters without offering any appreciable benefit.

The flexibility of the concept of national security is important for another reason. CFIUS's decisions can and do have a tangible and material impact on the foreign relations of the United States. I can tell you from experience that foreign embassies and governments take a very active interest in how their native companies are treated during the review process. It therefore is critically important that the CFIUS process reflect and complement the incumbent administration's broader foreign policy and national security priorities, within the parameters set by the Congress.

In practice, no administration has sought to adopt an explicit definition of national security for CFIUS purposes, instead leaving that determination to the agencies' discretion. The agencies' views, in turn, are influenced and shaped by the President's agenda. If Congress attempts to influence the definition of national security that CFIUS applies through additional mandatory reviews, investigations, or assessments, there is a danger that the Committee will find itself at cross purposes with the administration, leading to a less integrated, less cohesive foreign policy.

I share this background to help explain why I believe the flexibility of the language in FINSA and the CFIUS regulations is so critical to the Committee's proper functioning. I would urge the Commission to resist recommending any changes that would limit the Committee's discretion in defining national security for purposes of reviews. It is neither practical nor prudent to amend the CFIUS statute each time the national security landscape changes. We cannot predict what security risks our country will face in ten years, or even next year, and we should not try. Instead, we should recognize that it is the living language of the CFIUS statute that makes the institution most effective year after year.

Finally, I would suggest that the Commission and Congress consider whether CFIUS and the Agency staff that support the Committee would benefit from additional resources. As the number of investigations conducted by the committee has increased year-by-year, so too has the workload. I have witnessed firsthand the tireless efforts of the Committee's dedicated civil servants. These are not clock-watching bureaucrats; these men and women regularly work nights, weekends and holidays with little appreciation and no recognition, and often with a punishing caseload. Additional resources would promote the twin goals of protecting national security and promoting investment by ensuring that they have sufficient staff to evaluate transactions in a thorough and timely manner.

## B. State-controlled Entities and National Security

I recognize that investments from state-controlled entities, including state-owned enterprises ("SOEs") and sovereign wealth funds ("SWFs"), present unique challenges from a national security perspective. At the same time, these investors make valuable contributions to our economy. I would suggest to you that our national interests are best served if CFIUS is free to consider each such investment on a case-by-case basis and that additional statutory mandates targeted at SOEs and SWFs are both unnecessary and counterproductive.

There is always the possibility that a state-owned foreign investor may be motivated by political or national security considerations, rather than by purely commercial interests. At the same time, I believe that treating all entities with any form of government ownership stake or interest identically is unnecessary from a national security perspective, damaging to our economic interests, and will deservedly be seen as unfair by foreign observers.

SOEs are not a monolithic group. It is true that *some* SOEs are, in effect, organs of the state that operate with substantial direction from the government. Others are largely independent businesses with only incidental, historical or passive state ownership. And still others are in distinct phases of evolution on the continuum from state control to private control, with considerable conflict between the state and private stakeholders. To straitjacket all of these entities uniformly would be poor and unrefined policy.

If categorical protections are inadvisable, how then do we address the unique challenges that state-owned investors pose? I believe that we should require sufficient transparency from investors to permit CFIUS to make an informed decision about the risks of each individual transaction. The more transparent a corporation's governance and decision making, the more confidence we can have that its investments are motivated solely by business considerations. And, where there are credible risks, we can take appropriate steps to protect our security interests.

I note that, for transactions reviewed by CFIUS, we already demand an exceptional degree of transparency from investors, including SOEs. The CFIUS regulations require that all notices to the Committee contain a great deal of sensitive information. I can tell you from experience that foreign investors often are uncomfortable providing the level of detailed information sought by CFIUS. The foreign party is required to provide "Personal Identifier Information" about each and every officer and director, including date of birth, place of birth, "date and nature of foreign government and foreign military service," "national identity number, including nationality, date and place of issuance, and expiration date," and passport number, together with a detailed curriculum vitae.[7] The foreign party must also provide extensive information about its governance structure and ownership, including, where the ultimate parent is a public company, identifier information for any shareholder with an interest greater than five percent.[8] These data, once provided, are subjected to thorough analysis by CFIUS utilizing classified systems and databases.

In practice, some investors are simply unwilling to provide this information and self-select out of a potential transaction. Thus, by merely requiring this information, we reduce the pool of investors in the United States to those who are willing, at a minimum, to comply with our stringent information requirements. Moreover, state-controlled entities already are subject to additional scrutiny in the CFIUS process. Thus, FINSA creates a presumption that CFIUS will conduct an additional 45-day investigation for any transaction "that could result in control of a U.S. business by a foreign government or a person controlled by or acting on behalf of a foreign government."[9] This presumption may be overcome only if the Secretary of the Treasury and the head of the lead agency jointly determine ... that the transaction will not impair the national security of the United States."[10] The authority may not be delegated to anyone other than the Deputy Secretary of the Treasury or the equivalent in the lead agency.[11] My experience is that this discretionary authority is rarely, if ever, utilized to shorten a review process.

In my view, these policies represent an appropriate balancing of the need to protect our national security while at the same time encouraging foreign direct investment. The informational requirements operate as a "gatekeeping" mechanism that deters investors who are unwilling to subject themselves to the deep scrutiny required by CFIUS. Similarly, the additional review requirements for foreign government-controlled entities ensure that SOEs and SWFs receive appropriate scrutiny when they invest in the United States.

I urge the Commission not to recommend additional mandatory reviews for state-controlled entities. As I have noted, SOEs and SWFs are far from a monolithic group, and treating them as such penalizes responsible investors and contributes unnecessarily to the impression that the CFIUS process is arbitrary and unfair. It is worth recalling that foreign manufacturers — including from Japan, Germany, and China, among others — have created tens of thousands of U.S. manufacturing jobs without presenting appreciable national security threats. In the highly competitive mergers and acquisitions market, additional scrutiny and delay in CFIUS approval can be a crippling competitive disadvantage. To subject all state-controlled entities to such disadvantages diminishes the incentives for those foreign companies that have partial government ownership to be responsible and transparent in their management and ownership structures.

Instead, I believe that Congress and the administration should work with our allies and partners to promote good governance and improved transparency in state-controlled entities. Some significant efforts already are underway. The Organisation for Economic Cooperation and Development has published Guidelines on Corporate Governance of State-owned Enterprises, which lay out principles for how countries can more responsibly and transparently manage commercial enterprises in which they have a stake.[12] Similarly, the International Working Group of Sovereign Wealth Funds has established the "Sovereign Wealth Funds: Generally Accepted Principles and

Practices," commonly known as the "Santiago Principles."[13] These efforts demonstrate that some SOEs and SWFs are committed to transparency and responsible investment. The United States should encourage such responsible corporate behavior by rewarding those companies that embrace transparency and good governance.

In sum, it is true that investment by state-controlled entities raises unique national security challenges. Our national security review system already recognizes this risk and includes substantial provisions to ensure that such investors are scrutinized appropriately. Additional categorical requirements would serve only to punish responsible investors and distract from more pressing security concerns. As with other areas, my experience leads me to conclude that CFIUS functions most effectively when it is afforded the flexibility to consider each case on its own merits without being constrained by categorical mandates or requirements.

## C. State-owned Enterprises and Protection from Unfair Competition

As the Commission is well aware, the issues related to state-controlled enterprises are not limited to the implications for national security. Some SOEs receive substantial economic benefits from the state that threaten to distort markets and put American companies at an unfair disadvantage. But we are not powerless. The United States has a number of legal tools available to help promote a level playing field for U.S. businesses, including trade remedies and antitrust laws. I cannot say that these remedies are perfect or sufficient to neutralize the benefits received by Chinese SOEs. But I am confident that these laws and institutions — not CFIUS — are the appropriate mechanism by which to address the potential economic edge of Chinese SOEs.

China's membership in the WTO provides the United States with a number of legal options to remedy the effects of subsidies and other benefits provided to Chinese SOEs. The Agreement on Subsidies and Countervailing Measures ("SCM Agreement") specifically prohibits export subsidies, *i.e.*, any subsidies that are provided on condition of export or local content.[14] Subsidies that are not contingent on export may be actionable, (*i.e.*, subject to countervailing duties or challenge through the WTO's dispute settlement mechanism) if they are "specific," (meaning they are provided to one industry, such as SOEs), provide a "benefit," and cause "serious prejudice."[15]

Of course, these trade obligations only benefit U.S. businesses if they are enforced. Last year President Obama created the Interagency Trade Enforcement Center, led by the U.S. Trade Representative, to coordinate efforts across agencies to better monitor and enforce the United States' trade rights around the world.[16] This is a step in the right direction, but more work is needed. I encourage the Commission to consider whether the administration, and in particular USTR, has sufficient resources to enforce existing our trade rights and to protect U.S. businesses.

Our antitrust laws, which provide remedies for such practices as price fixing and predatory pricing, provide another opportunity to protect against unfair competition. Earlier this year, a federal jury returned a verdict against two Chinese companies for conspiring to raise the price of vitamin C exported to the United States, marking the first time that Chinese companies have faced trial in the United States under U.S antitrust law.[17] The companies defended on the basis that they were merely adhering to government-mandated volume and pricing restrictions, an argument the jury clearly rejected. The Court entered judgment for treble damages in the amount of $162.3 million. Another avenue the Commission could investigate is whether the Department of Justice and the Federal Trade Commission can take additional steps to pursue enforcement actions against Chinese business that violate our antitrust laws.

I offer these examples not to say that our existing competition and trade regimes are sufficient to entirely protect our economic interests. I do, however, submit that the trade and antitrust regimes are the correct mechanisms for protecting U.S. businesses and promoting a level playing field.

## II. CFIUS IS AN INAPPROPRIATE MECHANISM FOR ECONOMIC BENEFIT ASSESSMENT

That leads to me to my second key point. The CFIUS framework is ill suited to evaluating the economic effects of a transaction, such as through a net benefit test like that required by the Investment Canada Act.

First, the principles underlying the net benefit test diverge significantly from the core purpose of CFIUS, which is to evaluate whether a transaction threatens to impair national security and take action, as necessary, to protect our security interests. The Committee's statutes, regulations, membership, policies, and procedures all revolve around this essential function. For this reason the Departments of Defense and Homeland Security are typically two of the most influential agencies in the Committee process. The professional CFIUS staff itself within the Department of the Treasury is relatively small and primarily serves a coordinating role. While highly sophisticated, I do not believe that this staff itself has the capacity to conduct the complex economic analysis that would be necessary to support a net benefit test.

Instead, we have entire departments and agencies full of talented economists, diplomats, and regulators whose mission is to promote a level playing field for U.S. businesses. They work for the Office of the U.S. Trade Representative, the Federal Trade Commission, the International Trade Commission, the Department of State, and the Department of Justice's Antitrust Division.

Second, CFIUS operates under an exceptionally rare amount of secrecy for a regulatory agency. All submissions are confidential and protected from public disclosure. The Committee's orders are not made public and it is not required to make any public report or explanation of its decision in any particular case. There is no opportunity for public hearing and, as was recently confirmed, the Committee's decisions are not subject to judicial review. This secrecy is essential to protect not only the national security interests of the United States, but also the highly sensitive personal and business information that is submitted to the Committee. I submit that such lack of transparency is inappropriate to the conduct of an economic benefit test and would risk devolving into unprincipled protectionism — or, at a minimum, would be perceived as such. If we are to have a mechanism to review the economic benefits of transactions, it should be transparent and subject to public scrutiny.

Finally, Canada's experience also cautions against adoption of a net benefit test. Although some support the idea of a net benefit test in principle, nearly every Canadian political party seems to agree that they do not care for it in practice, albeit for different reasons. Opponents criticize the test as unnecessary, inconsistent with free trade and investment, and lacking in intelligible standards. Supporters, on the other hand, lament that the power to block transactions has been used only twice. Recently, the Canadian government has increased the threshold amount to qualify a transaction for review under the test to $1 billion, from $330 million, reflecting in part the reality that the measure has been controversial and difficult to apply in practice.

## III. The Interrelation of National Security and Foreign Investment

The final point I wish to make concerns the interrelation of foreign investment and national security. Some of the policy proposals I hear considered seem to assume that national security and foreign investment are zero sum calculations; that is, an increase in foreign investment necessarily leads to a correlative decline in our national security. This simply is not the case. We need not sacrifice valuable investment to protect our security interests, nor must we risk our national security in order to welcome investment. Both are worthy ends that can and should be pursued simultaneously and with equal vigor.

Our nation has a longstanding policy of openness to foreign investment. In May 2007, President George W. Bush issued a statement on the United States' openness toward foreign investment, called a statement on "Open Economies."[18] In the wake of the Dubai Ports World controversy, the Bush Administration sought to reassure the world that the United States remained open to foreign direct investment. Similar policy statements were made by Presidents Carter, Reagan, and George H.W. Bush.[19] And in 2011, President Obama released a statement on the "United States Commitment to Open Investment Policy" that "reaffirms our open investment policy, a commitment to treat all investors in a fair and equitable manner under the law."[20]

There is good reason for this rare, longstanding, bi-partisan consensus. Clear and convincing evidence shows that foreign direct investment contributes to a stronger manufacturing base, creates higher paying jobs, promotes investment in domestic research and development, and generates greater tax revenue. The White House Council of Economic Advisors has reported that U.S. affiliates of foreign companies in 2008 produced $670 billion in goods and services, 42 percent of which is concentrated in the manufacturing sector, and employed 5.7 million U.S. workers, or about five percent of the U.S. private workforce.[21]

The United States traditionally has been the world's premier investment location, with twice as much foreign direct investment comes here as compared to second-ranked China in 2011. But our share of global foreign direct investment has dropped rapidly, from 37 percent in 2000 to 17 percent in 2011, due in large part to companies' shifting capital to fast-growing developing countries like China.[22] These figures should be a caution to those considering additional requirements on foreign investors.

With the increasingly competitive market for foreign direct investment in mind, I want to address in particular the idea of applying reciprocity requirements to our trade and investment laws. Such a policy would, in effect, require that the United States deny the right to invest in the United States to countries that do not extend the same rights to U.S. companies. This argument fundamentally misapprehends the nature of foreign investment. Foreign direct investment benefits the United States regardless of whether U.S. companies are extended equivalent access to foreign markets.

This does not mean that we should not advocate vigorously and aggressively to open markets overseas to investment by U.S. businesses. We should. But to make approval for foreign investment contingent on reciprocity would unnecessarily deny the United States the benefits of foreign investment and risk additional tightening of international investment regimes. We should keep in mind that our national security review process is itself more restrictive than its counterparts in many of our most important trading partners and closest allies, some of whom have no formal process for evaluating the national security risk of foreign investment. Requiring reciprocity in our laws and policies — even if limited to China — I believe would risk subjecting U.S. businesses to similar requirements when they invest abroad.

* * *

Encouraging foreign investment, protecting our national security, and ensuring a level playing field for U.S. businesses are all worthy and important policy goals. Fortunately, they also are goals that can be pursued simultaneously. I would encourage the Commission to resist the temptation to recommend additional statutory mandates for our national security review process. It is the flexibility to review each transaction on a case-by-case basis that makes CFIUS effective. Instead, I encourage the Commission to consider how it can help empower CFIUS and our other institutions through additional resources.

Thank you again for the opportunity to address the Commission. I would be happy to take your questions.

## End Notes

[1] Mark E. Plotkin is a partner in the law firm Covington & Burling LLP in Washington, D.C. His practice encompasses foreign investment and national security, financial services, and data privacy matters. This testimony represents the personal views of Mr. Plotkin and is not

offered on behalf of any client or of his firm. Mr. Plotkin can be contacted by email at mplotkin@cov.com or by telephone at (202) 662-5656.

[2] See Foreign Investment and National Security Act, 50 U.S.C. App. § 2170 (b)(1)(A)(i) (2012).

[3] 50 U.S.C. App. § 2170 (a)(5).

[4] 50 U.S.C. App. § 2170 (f).

[5] 31 CFR § 800.

[6] § 800.402(c)(3)(viii).

[7] § 800.402(c)(6)(vi).

[8] Id.

[9] 50 U.S.C. App. § 2170 (b)(2)(B)(i)(III).

[10] 50 U.S.C. App. § 2170 (b)(2)(D)(i).

[11] Id.

[12] Organisation for Economic Cooperation and Development, OECD Guidelines on Corporate Governance of State-owned Enterprises (2005), available at http://www.oecd.org/corporate/ca/corporategovernanceofstateownedenterprises/34803211.pdf.

[13] International Working Group of Sovereign Wealth Funds, "Generally Accepted Principles and Practices (Oct. 2008), available at http://www.iwg-swf.org/pubs/eng/santiagoprinciples.pdf.

[14] WTO Agreement on Subsidies and Countervailing Measures ("SCM Agreement"), art. 3.

[15] SCM Agreement, art. 2.

[16] See Press Release, The White House, "Executive Order -- Establishment of the Interagency Trade Enforcement Center" (Feb. 28, 2012).

[17] See In re: Vitamin C Antitrust Litigation (E.D.N.Y. 2012).

[18] Press Release, The White House, President Bush's Statement on Open Economies (May 10, 2007), available at http://2001-2009.state.gov/e/eeb/rls/prsrl/2007/84660.htm.

[19] James Jackson, "Foreign direct investment: current issues," Congressional Research Service Report to Congress, April 27, 2007, at 6-7 (internal citation omitted).

[20] Press Release, The White House, Statement by the President on United States Commitment to Open Investment Policy (June 20, 2011), available at http://www.whitehouse.gov/the-press-office/2011/06/20/statementpresident-united-states-commitment-open-investment-policy.

[21] Executive Office of the President, Council of Economic Advisors, "U.S. Inbound Foreign Direct Investment" (June 2011), available at http://www.whitehouse.gov/sites/ default/files/microsites/cea_fdi_report.pdf.

[22] Organization for International Investment, Foreign Direct Investment in the United States: 2012 Preliminary Data (Mar. 20, 2013), available at http://www.ofii.org/docs/ FDIUS_2012_Annual_Data.pdf.

# INDEX

## A



## B

## D



## E

## H



## I



## J



## K

## T